# 101 *Glimpses of* Nags Head

# 101 *Glimpses of* Nags Head

Sarah Downing

The History Press

Published by The History Press
Charleston, SC 29403
www.historypress.net



First published 2009

Manufactured in the United States

ISBN 978.1.59629.607.7

Library of Congress Cataloging-in-Publication Data

Downing, Sarah.
101 glimpses of Nags Head / Sarah Downing.
p. cm.
ISBN 978-1-59629-607-7
1. Nags Head (N.C.)--History--Pictorial works. 2. Nags Head (N.C.)--Social life and customs--Pictorial works. I. Title. II. Title: One hundred and one glimpses of Nags Head. III. Title: One hundred one glimpses of Nags Head.
F264.N3D69 2009
975.6'175--dc22
2009013738

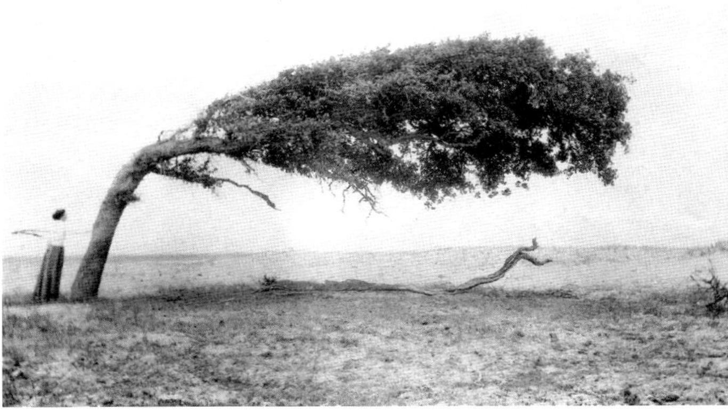

*The blowing sand which borders sea*
*And covers all—so let it be—*
*I hope in time it covers me*
*At old Nag's Head*

*From "A Pinch of Salt" by Thomas J. Nixon III*

# CONTENTS

# ACKNOWLEDGEMENTS

Working on a local history book takes the efforts and contributions of many. I would like to thank the following people who helped by providing photos, technical assistance and information to help to tell the story.

Alison, Barb, Doug and Pat at Coastal Impressions
Jimmy and Sandra Austin, Austin's Seafood
George Barnes, Jockey's Ridge State Park
Billy Brown
Tama Creef, Outer Banks History Center
Kim Cumber, North Carolina State Archives
Tom Dugan, *Eastern Surf Magazine*
Glenn and Pat Eure, Ghost Fleet Gallery
Bob Furr, photographer
Jennifer Gilbreath, Nags Head Woods Preserve
Larry Gray, Gray's Sportswear
Steve Hess, Secret Spot Surf Shop
Randell Holmes

Claudia Jew, Mariners' Museum
Jim Lee, photographer
Keith Longiotti, North Carolina Collection, University of North Carolina–Chapel Hill
Lisa Loy, photographer
Joe Martone
Mickey McCarthy
Roger P. Meekins, photographer
Lynda Midgett
Stuart Parks II, Outer Banks History Center
Jason Powell, National Park Service
Pat Preston
Budgie and Anna Sadler
Jack Sandberg
Ronnie Scott
Dakota Seegers, Secret Spot Surf Shop
Carol Sykes and the crew at Sam and Omie's
The Slaytons, Cavalier Surf Shop
Chester Smith, Seaside Art Gallery
Melanie Smith, Seaside Art Gallery
KaeLi Spiers, Outer Banks History Center
Jim and April Vaughn, Whalebone Surf Shop
Laurin Walker, *Eastern Surf Magazine*
Karen Wartliner, Kelly's Restaurant and Tavern
Alan Westmoreland, North Carolina State Archives
Sylvia Williams
Drew C. Wilson, photographer
Chaz Winkler, Beachcomber Museum

# INTRODUCTION

## Early History

Nags Head has the distinction of having been a resort long before the other areas of North Carolina's Outer Banks. As early as the 1830s, merchants and planters from the Albemarle region of North Carolina and Southside Virginia brought their families to Nags Head via boat to escape the oppressive summer heat inland and to take advantage of ocean breezes, sea bathing and the general healthy climate. These stays were long, and visitors brought everything they would need for an extended vacation—furniture, tutors, servants and livestock.

George Higby Throop, writing under the name of Gregory Seaworthy, penned a fictional account of his stay at Nags Head as a tutor for a wealthy family prior to the Civil War:

> *The resort was soon thronged. A hotel was built, and a chapel. Roads were cut through the woods, and among*

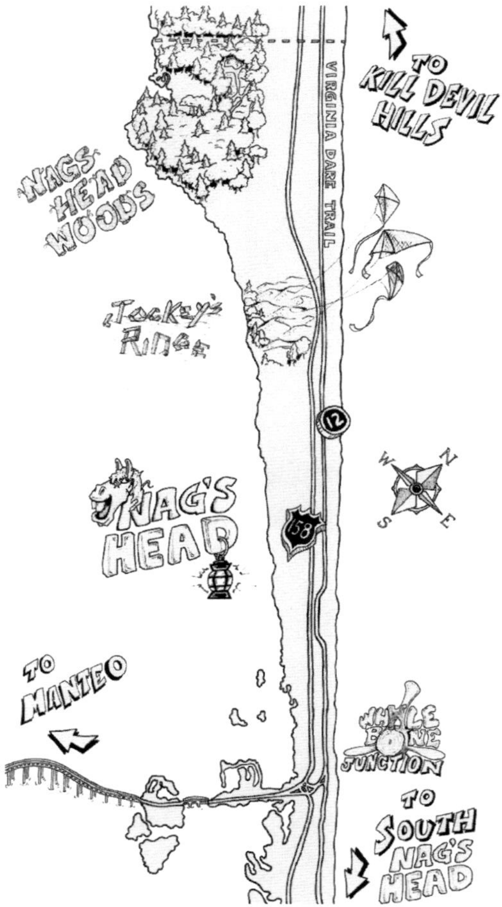


Map of Nags Head, North Carolina. Legend has it that land pirates would drape a lantern over the head of a nag and then walk the horse over the dunes. At sea, ships would assume the light was another ship on the ocean and would sail too close to shore, where the stranded vessel was plundered. *Map by Stuart Parks II.*

> *what the bankers call "the up-guoines" (sand-hills). The song and the dance; the fox-hunt, the bowling-alley, and the delicious fish were powerful recommendations, and Nag's Head became but another name for happiness. Lovers walked on the sea-shore. Doctors practiced without fees. It was respectable to be seen in homespun.*

Unlike many other seaside resorts, Nags Head was largely composed of privately owned homes. Families, friends and neighbors vacationed amongst one another. This gathering place for the well-to-do was very much a social climate where relationships were forged that would last generations.

During the Civil War, General Wise of Virginia made his headquarters at Nags Head, bringing men and supplies down the beach from Princess Anne County, Virginia, or by a ferry near the site of the present-day Wright Memorial Bridge. Wise suffered high fever and an attack of pleurisy and was too sick to command his troops. He would lose his son, O. Jennings Wise of the Richmond Light Infantry Blues, at the Battle of Roanoke Island in February 1862. Before retreating with a contingent of his men, the hotel in which he had made his headquarters was burned and much personal property was destroyed so that it would not fall into enemy hands.

After the war, it wasn't long before families once again began to summer at Nags Head. The original resort was located on the sound side, where families and their belongings arrived on sloops and steamers that landed at long docks extending into the sound or anchored off shore, where passengers were ferried ashore in smaller boats. Later cottages were built on the oceanfront. Mrs. C.W. Hollowell, née Parthenia Gatling, wrote of her early experiences in Nags Head for a column in the Elizabeth City *Daily Advance* in 1933:

> *In the spring of 1868 my father, James Lawrence Gatling, of Cedar Vale in Perquimans County near Hertford, decided he would build a cottage on the ocean side at Nags Head. So he bought an acre from Francis Nixon the elder, paying $25.00 for the lot. The timber was cut and prepared for the house just as it was to be set up on arrival on the site at Nags Head. Every piece of lumber was so planned and adjusted that there was nothing to do but put it together. Early in July everything was ready for the family to go down and take possession.*
>
> *My father chartered a large seagoing vessel, the* Georgia, *to take us and our household furnishings also a horse and two carts, one large one for hauling purposes and a neat painted spring cart to drive about in.*

In addition to her family's oceanfront house, Hollowell attributes early oceanfront cottages to Dr. William G. Pool, George D. Pool, Reuben Overman, C. Wiley Grandy, William Griffin and Isaiah Fearing of Elizabeth City and James Sumner from Perquimans County.

Although the advent of the automobile was spurring road construction in some parts of the country, Nags Head continued as an isolated destination accessible only by boat well into the twentieth century. In 1927, Washington Baum from Manteo hatched a plan to connect Roanoke Island with Nags Head by constructing a causeway and a bridge over the Roanoke Sound. Although many thought his idea frivolous, as well as a waste of money, Baum knew that if a bridge was built, roads would surely follow.

Soon afterward, a group of businessmen from Elizabeth City and the Albemarle area bought a large tract of land in Kitty Hawk and built the Wright Memorial Bridge from Point Harbor to Kitty Hawk. Sure enough, the State of North Carolina came through and built a paved road that connected these two bridges.

Inns, tourist homes, cottage courts, hotels and other businesses began to appear along the Virginia Dare Trail, often referred to today as the Beach Road. Nags Head was now easier to reach, as were its virtues. People would come to hunt, fish, enjoy the beaches, take in the beautiful scenery and visit the historic attractions nearby.

## JOCKEY'S RIDGE AND THE DUNES

Ever since the earliest visitors came to enjoy Nags Head, they have enjoyed the shifting sand dunes that make up most of the landscape. A series of sand hills ran from Kill

Devil Hill and Run Hill south to Jockey's Ridge, followed by Engagement Hill and the Seven Sisters. Closer to Oregon Inlet was Wreck Hill. Jockey's Ridge, however, was the tallest dune system and was adjacent to the original soundside resort.

By the 1950s, the meandering sands that made up Jockey's Ridge were owned by several different parties, with property lines winding over the rolling hills, and for years no one gave much thought to who owned them. They were there, as they had been for years, for the public to use and enjoy. But as development on the Outer Banks began to pick up, community leaders saw a need to preserve Jockey's Ridge.

In 1964, David Stick was elected chairman of the Nags Head Chamber of Commerce, and he suggested that a goal during his term would be to work toward public acquisition of Jockey's Ridge. Obstacles arose, such as determining ownership of the various tracts of land and convincing known landowners to sell out at a time when the price of real estate was on the rise.

Fast forward to 1972, when Jim High of Rocky Mount began to develop the northwest portion of Jockey's Ridge as the Villas condominium project. Locals Henry Applewhite and Phillip Quidley, calling themselves Friends of Jockey's Ridge, sent a telegram to movers and shakers in North Carolina. These two men should be given due credit for their efforts, for they were the first to organize and the first to inform the outside world of the destruction that was taking place at the most well-known landmark in Nags Head.

Enter Walter and Carolista Fletcher Baum. Carolista has long been viewed as the poster child for the Save Our Sand Dunes movement. After seeing firsthand the demolition of Jockey's Ridge, the Baums mobilized to save it. Carolista and Walter formed a new preservation group, the People to Preserve Jockey's Ridge. Carolista enthusiastically devoted her time and energy to a cause in which she thoroughly believed. Additional support came from the Town of Nags Head, which passed a resolution in 1972 requesting the North Carolina Department of Conservation and Development, the North Carolina Division of State Parks and the State of North Carolina to consider the feasibility of preserving Jockey's Ridge as a state park.

Informational booths were set up in Nags Head and at the Christmas Shop in Manteo. T-shirts, kites and other promotional items were sold. Money was collected in donation boxes. Deeds "selling" a square foot of the dune could be purchased for a five-dollar contribution, and foundations were solicited for donations, as were wealthy individuals across North Carolina.

Money was also appropriated in Raleigh for the acquisition of portions of the dunes. Tracts were purchased as well as donated, and in 1975, Jockey's Ridge became a part of the North Carolina State Park System.

Jockey's Ridge State Park now hosts over one million visitors each year who come to hike the dunes, fly kites, picnic, enjoy the sound-side beach and commune with nature. The staff offers free educational programming on a wide variety of topics.

## NAGS HEAD WOODS

About the same time that Jockey's Ridge was made a state park, another natural treasure in Nags Head was also protected, but this time by the Nature Conservancy. In fact, it was after a nomination by the People to Preserve Jockey's Ridge that Nags Head Woods was named a National Natural Landmark by the U.S. Department of the Interior.

Nags Head Woods is an ecologically unique maritime forest and, as such, is home to over three hundred plant species (some of which are classified as rare) and fifty bird species, along with mammals, reptiles and amphibians.

While Nags Head was developing as a resort, native families lived in the woods in homes built high on its ridges. People existed by fishing, hunting, gardening and foraging for berries, grapes and chinquapins that the woods environment provided. Until 1937, livestock roamed free, subsisting on acorns and marsh grasses. They were corralled in the spring, when new calves were branded. Lumber was milled from the woods or salvaged from shipwrecks along with other goods. In the early 1900s, the community was large enough to support two churches and a school.

As change came to the Outer Banks, it came to Nags Head Woods. Selling vegetables, berries, soft crabs and fresh meat to the summer people became a way to supplement income, as well as caring for cottages in the off-season or providing domestic services in the summer. During World War I, men left for jobs. Women married and moved away. The school closed in the 1930s. The last woods residents were gone by the 1950s.

Nags Head Woods is interspersed with several freshwater ponds, including the largest, the Fresh Pond, which straddles the Nags Head–Kill Devil Hills town line and was for many years the main source of fresh water for both municipalities. Before protection, the Fresh Pond was a favorite fishing spot. Indian artifacts have been found on its shores.

George Higby Throop mentioned the popularity of the ponds in his 1850 novel, *Nag's Head, or, Two Months among "The Bankers"*: "On almost any day in August or September, you might have found half a score of resolute anglers, patiently plying their taciturn vocation in the shade of overhanging trees."

After Nags Head Woods was named a National Natural Landmark in 1974, the Nature Conservancy placed the maritime forest high on its list of priorities for preservation. In the following years, bits and pieces of land were acquired through purchase, donation and agreements with the Towns of Nags Head and Kill Devil Hills.

Today the woods comprise over one thousand acres administered by the North Carolina Nature Conservancy and are now known as the Nags Head Woods Ecological Preserve. For the past twenty-five years the area has been the site of the annual Nags Head Woods Run, which draws over four hundred participants, young and old, from North Carolina, Virginia and mid-Atlantic states.

## THE U.S. LIFE-SAVING SERVICE AND THE U.S. COAST GUARD

It is impossible to explain the presence in Nags Head of the United States Life-saving Service, and later the United States Coast Guard, without providing some background to put things in an appropriate historic perspective.

The United States has a rich maritime history. As the country developed, so did its port towns. Goods were shipped on sloops and schooners, and a brisk maritime trade began to develop by the early 1800s. However, as long as there were ships, there would also be shipwrecks. Because navigational aids were in their infancy, ships tended to stick close to shore using day marks to maintain their bearings. This put ships in danger of running aground and stranding. Once grounded, a ship was at risk of breaking up and putting the lives of passengers and crew in peril.

Efforts to provide respite for stranded mariners and passengers first became apparent around the busy ports of New York and Boston. As early as 1785, the Massachusetts Humane Society provided houses of refuge, simple structures containing food or clothing that could be used as shelter for stranded seamen. Other attempts to provide assistance to shipwreck victims were inadequate and were based on the efforts of volunteers.

The federal government first appropriated money in 1837 for ships of the U.S. Revenue Cutter Service to offer assistance to ships at sea during the winter season. In 1848, New Jersey congressman William A. Newell championed for lifesaving efforts by urging Congress to appropriate funds for the construction of lifesaving stations and the procurement of lifesaving equipment. While stations were funded and constructed by the federal government, they were handed over to local communities to operate via volunteers.

The catastrophic loss of life and property during a fierce storm in 1854 again drew attention to the need to advance lifesaving efforts along the coast. Congress again appropriated funds, but this time it called for the employment of station keepers. The first manned stations were found along the coast of New Jersey and Long Island.

While the Civil War more or less brought a halt to this progress, another terrible storm in 1870 further drew focus on the need for improvements. In 1871, a lifesaving branch was established under the U.S. Revenue Cutter Service, and a new superintendent, Sumner I. Kimball, began to evaluate and assess operations and how to improve upon them.

Seven lifesaving stations were built along the Outer Banks in 1874, including one at Nags Head. These 1874 stations were one-and-a-half-story, nineteen- by forty-three-foot buildings and were characterized by ornate exterior trim and a watchtower on top of the center of the building. The stations were manned by a keeper and a crew of six men for the four-month active season that ran from December to March. In 1912, a second station was built at Nags Head in what was known as the Chicamacomico style.

Many men from Nags Head, the Outer Banks and other coastal counties gained employment with the Life-saving Service, sometimes transferring from one station to another to move up in the ranks.

When on patrol, a crewman would walk the beach looking for any distressed ships or act to ensure that a disaster was averted. Often a ship was spotted too close to shore, and a Coston's flare was burned to signal the ship at sea. The captain could then steer clear of any danger and move toward deeper water and away from breaking waves. The patrolman might hear a ship's bell or whistle as a signal of thanks.

On those occasions when a ship did run aground or, worse yet, break up in the waves, the patrolman would head back to the station and report the incident to the station keeper, who would summon the crew to perform a rescue. If additional help was needed, a second station would be alerted and that crew would also respond. The crew of the Bodie Island Station worked alongside the Nags Head crew many times.

Sometimes surfmen could wade out to assist passengers; at other times a line was fired out to a ship and secured by someone onboard. Passengers and crew could then use the line as a guide to make it back to shore. Another method of rescue was using a breeches buoy, a contraption that was a life preserver with a seat in it. A line was fired and attached to a ship, and the breeches buoy was then hauled out using a rope and pulley system. The stranded passengers and crew would sit in the breeches buoy one by one to be hauled ashore. If a wreck was far from shore, a lifeboat was launched to perform rescues.

The worst known shipwreck off Nags Head was the disaster of the USS *Huron* in November 1877, which took place just five years after the formation of the U.S. Life-saving Service, when the active season was only four months long. After a stop at Hampton Roads on its itinerary from New York to Cuba, the man-of-war struck ground off Nags Head in fog and high seas early on the morning of November 24. Men aboard the *Huron* were washed overboard by ferocious waves as the dark hours waned into daybreak. The Nags Head Life-saving Station, less than three miles south of the stranding, was unmanned and locked. Locals saw flares of distress sent out from the *Huron* but were afraid to break into the government-owned station, and even if they had, they didn't know how to use the equipment housed there.

The disaster took the lives of 103 men, 98 from the *Huron* and another 5 in a rescue party. The devastating loss caused newspaper editors to cry out for more adequate coverage by the U.S. Life-saving Service. The active season was extended from September to May and later from August 1 to May 31. Additionally, crews were expanded from 6 to 7 men.

The U.S. Life-saving Service merged with the U.S. Revenue Cutter Service in 1915 as the United States Coast Guard. The Nags Head Station was transferred to the General Services Administration in 1957, but it suffered irreparable damage in the Ash Wednesday Storm of March 1962. The Bodie Island Station was transferred to the National Park Service in 1953 and is now on the National Register of Historic Places.

A new facility, Coast Guard Station Oregon Inlet, was built on the north side of the inlet in 1990 and annually responds to over two hundred requests for assistance to mariners.

## OUR FISHING CULTURE

Fishing helped to sustain Nags Head's earliest residents as well as providing them with a seasonal income, or at least a commodity with which to barter. The 1900 census lists fisherman as the chief occupation for Nags Headers. Nets were launched in dories and pulled in by hand and later by truck. Some fish were salted down, while fresh fish could be shipped to dealers in Norfolk, Baltimore, Philadelphia and New York.

Although commercial net fishing from the beach does not constitute a large industry, the Town of Nags Head Land Use Plan provides for the protection of this traditional livelihood that has been part of the culture for hundreds of years.

## *Nags Head Surf Fishing Tournament*

As the area developed as a vacation destination, recreational fishermen discovered the lure of surf fishing from Nags Head's beaches. It was the popularity of fishing, combined with a desire to create an event to draw visitors during the off-season, that brought about the creation of the Nags Head Surf Fishing Tournament.

By the 1950s, the post–World War II boom in tourism had taken hold in Nags Head. Hotels and businesses had sprung up along the Virginia Dare Trail, and entrepreneurs were making a go of it. Visitors, however, seemed to flock to the beaches only during the summer months. Local anglers knew that the fall was the time when the fish began to bite. In an effort to create an off-season draw, Jim Scarborough, Leo Murphy, Warren Jennette, Dal Williams and Dan Harris came up with an idea.

They formed the Nags Head Surf Fishing Club and began to organize the Nags Head Surf Fishing Tournament. The Carolinian Hotel sponsored a tournament in 1951, and the Nags Head Surf Fishing Club took the reins the following year and thereafter. The first tournament was headquartered at Jennette's Pier, with teams from a dozen states participating.

The tournament continues each October, a Nags Head tradition. Currently, eighty teams take part in the annual invitational event, while several teams are on a waiting list if a spot opens up.

### *The Piers*

In 1939, Warren Jennette built Jennette's Fishing Pier at the southern end of Nags Head. Gaston Mann followed in 1947, when he built Mann's Ocean Pier, now known as Nags Head Pier. George Thurman wrote in recollections of his youth that Mann was a muscular man, not afraid of hard work. Thurman recalled Mann cutting off each piling that had been driven into the ocean floor and notching them himself. By 1959, Nags Head could boast of three fishing piers when Red Mitchell from West Virginia opened the Seaport Pier in South Nags Head, known today as Outer Banks Pier.

The piers have all suffered storm damage over the years and have been patched and rebuilt many times. Jennette's Pier was destroyed after Hurricane Isabel in 2003, and the pier house was removed in 2008. Under the auspices of the North Carolina Aquarium Society, the pier will be rebuilt.

## OUR SURF CULTURE

By 1966, Nags Head was mentioned in *Atlantic Surfing Magazine* when a group of young Virginia Beach surfers were photographed surfing Nags Head waves and given a brief write-up. In addition to trickling down from Virginia Beach, some Nags Head surfers were college students who came to wait tables and earn money during the summer, surfing during their free time. Local surfers were made up of kids whose parents ran businesses on the beach or teens from Manteo and Wanchese.

### *Whalebone Surf Shop*

In 1975, Florida native Jim Vaughn and an out-of-town partner opened Resincraft Surf Shop in an eight-hundred-square-foot building next to Holy Trinity Catholic Church at Whalebone Junction. The following year, he bought out his associate and changed the name to Whalebone Junction Surf Shop.

Vaughn fashioned a living area in the attic of the building and was consequently never late for work. As the Outer Banks were much more seasonal then, Whalebone Junction Surf Shop opened in the late spring and closed in November, or according to Vaughn, "when the water reached fifty-eight degrees."

Along with surf wear, which in those days consisted of Hang Ten, Ocean Pacific and Sun Decks, Whalebone Junction Surf Shop also carried Levi jeans and Sperry shoes. After returning from a long fishing trip and getting paid, and prior to going to Sam and Omie's for food and drink, trawl boat workers would stop in the shop and often buy a few articles of clothing. Other times, captains or mates from Oregon Inlet or Wanchese would bring Vaughn fish. These gestures were helpful to the fledgling business. He says he ended up with just what he was looking for—"small-town atmosphere and good surf."

In 1983, Vaughn married April Clough and also opened up a 1,400-square-foot shop in Outer Banks Mall. April gave up her real estate career the following year and became a partner in the business. It was after the opening of the second store that the shop became known as simply Whalebone Surf Shop. The original Whalebone Junction store closed in 1985.

Over the years, the Vaughns operated several stores in various locations up and down the Outer Banks. Their current Nags Head store was built in 1990 at milepost 9.5 on the Bypass. They also operate a shop in Virginia Beach.

### *Secret Spot Surf Shop*

Steve Hess grew up coming to the Outer Banks to visit friends and family. It was a short drive from his home in Norfolk. Hess began surfing in 1968 on one of his brothers' ten-foot Bob White surfboards. In the late '60s, he "started fooling around with shaping" after watching Pete Manuel, a neighborhood garage shaper. Hess shaped his first board for a friend in the early 1970s. After his parents opened Captain Frank's Hotdogs in Kitty Hawk in 1975, Hess spent most of his time on the Outer Banks.

After mastering some basics of shaping, Hess traveled to Puerto Rico and learned more under the tutelage of Monte Smith of Island Surfboards. He returned to Kitty Hawk and began shaping boards with Mike Price under the name Secret Spot in 1977.

Back then, he says, "the whole northern banks was known as Nags Head, no one said lets go to Kill Devil Hills or Kitty Hawk it was just plain Nags Head." In 1982, he opened Secret Spot Surf Shop on the Bypass at milepost 11, which has become a landmark for being the oldest surf shop under the same name and owner at the same location. "The main challenge of a surf shop then was just to make enough money to stay open."

Secret Spot Surf Shop was one of the sponsors and organizers of the Surf Classic and Beach Bash held in Nags Head in 1987 and 1988. The event—which featured a surfing contest, a volleyball tournament behind the Atlantis nightclub and an after party at the Atlantis—was a fundraiser for Outer Banks Hotline and the Nags Head Fire Department.

While he still owns Secret Spot Surf Shop, which is run by a handful of trusted employees, Hess now lives overseas on a small island with friendly people and consistent waves where surfing is still in its infancy. He admits, however, that the area near Secret Spot "is forever carved into my heart."

### *New Sun Surfboards*

Virginia Beach native Mickey McCarthy, who had worked for Wave Riding Vehicles, moved to the Outer Banks with his wife in 1981. He found a small shop on the Beach Road and began shaping boards under the name New Sun

Surfboards. These were wonderful and formative years, although McCarthy admits he didn't realize it at the time.

Early on, he met up with Murray Ross, who had done some ding repair (patching dents and holes in fiberglass boards) under the Nags Header Hotel in the late 1960s and early 1970s when he was employed there as a short-order cook. Ross moved on to shaping boards at his Nags Head home. Both men were hands-on type of craftsmen who enjoyed building and creating. McCarthy's specialty was short boards, while Ross preferred long boards. They worked together for many years and were responsible for teaching a new generation of young shapers.

In its prime, New Sun was producing one thousand boards a year. A true grass-roots surf shop, it was never looking to mass produce boards. While the shop never advertised, word of mouth was enough to generate orders for New Sun Surfboards. Friends of Ross from New York started ordering boards. Then a shop in Bethany Beach, Delaware, carried them, along with shops in Ships Bottom, New Jersey; Long Beach, New York; and Hull, Massachusetts. Even an "artsy shop" in Greenwich Village carried them. McCarthy says it was an odd feeling "driving through Manhattan with a bunch of surfboards on your truck."

New Sun was at its Beach Road location for about ten years. As the company grew, shapers often worked late at night. Around 1990, town officials pointed out that manufacturing surfboards was against zoning regulations.

According to McCarthy, "The town couldn't have been nicer." In fact, several town employees were surfers who rode New Sun boards.

Consequently, New Sun became the first business in the Ocean Commerce Park in southern Kill Devil Hills. The owners got a corner unit and crafted a two-story shop. McCarthy retired in 2000. The shop continues today as Gale Force Glass with Murray Ross and Rascoe Hunt at the helm.

### *Cavalier Surf Shop*

The concrete block Cavalier Surf Shop was probably built in the mid- to late 1950s. It was run by a Mrs. Gregory when the combination surf shop/launderette was sold to Virginia Beach's Ken and Marty Slayton in 1986.

The original shop didn't sell much surfing equipment but instead rented umbrellas and chairs to tourists. Marty remembers doing laundry for the waiters and waitresses from Sea Fare, Papagayo and Penguin Isle. Even though two sets of sliding barn doors were left open, the shop was "hotter than hell."

The laundry service was discontinued, and the Slaytons beefed up their offerings and began to carry boards by Mike Fehmel and Mike Price's Hot and Nasty boards that featured a logo of girls "with less than a swimming suit."

The Cavalier also began selling used boards in the winter, when locals would come in and sell their old boards. This collection became the "rental fleet" that would be rented out, but they "were glass and the boards always came back dinged."

Fourth of July parties were popular annual events, and Midnight Madness sales from 9:00 p.m. to midnight were so packed that you couldn't turn around. The Cavalier continues to be a happening shop, in part due to Jerry Slayton, Ken and Marty's affable son.

Chapter 1

# EARLY NAGS HEAD

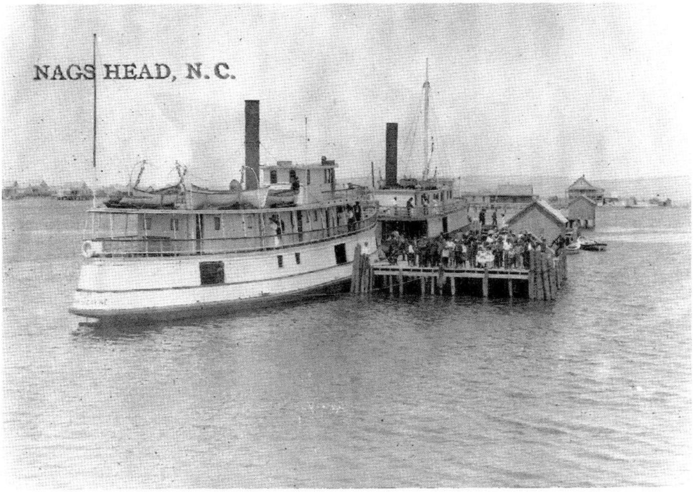


Early on, ships stopping at Nags Head moored out in the sound, as the water adjacent to the resort was too shallow for large craft. Passengers and their belongings were ferried ashore in smaller vessels. In 1852, the first wharf was built out into the sound, allowing passengers to disembark directly. *North Carolina Collection, University of North Carolina at Chapel Hill, circa 1930.*

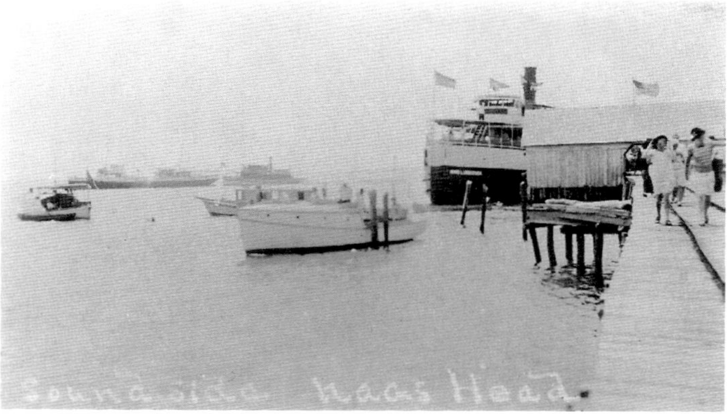


From the mid-1920s to the mid-1930s, the *Annie L. Vansciever* plied the waters of the Albemarle Sound, moving goods to and from Nags Head on Tuesdays and Thursdays and taking excursionists from Elizabeth City to Nags Head on Sundays. The steamer *Trenton* stopped at Nags Head on its run from Elizabeth City to Manteo. *Brant Wise Collection, Outer Banks History Center, circa 1930.*

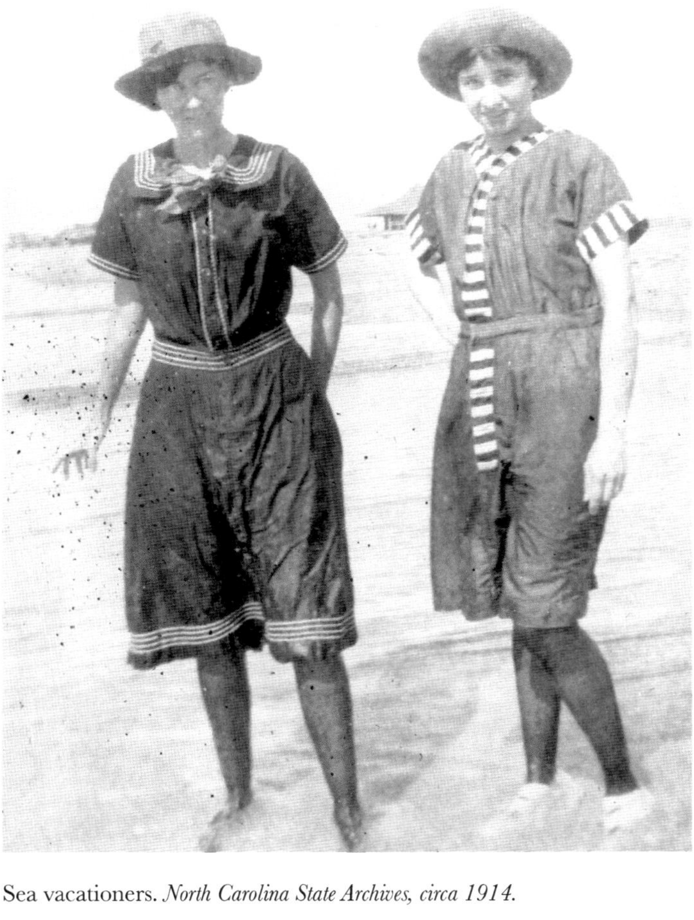

Sea vacationers. *North Carolina State Archives, circa 1914.*

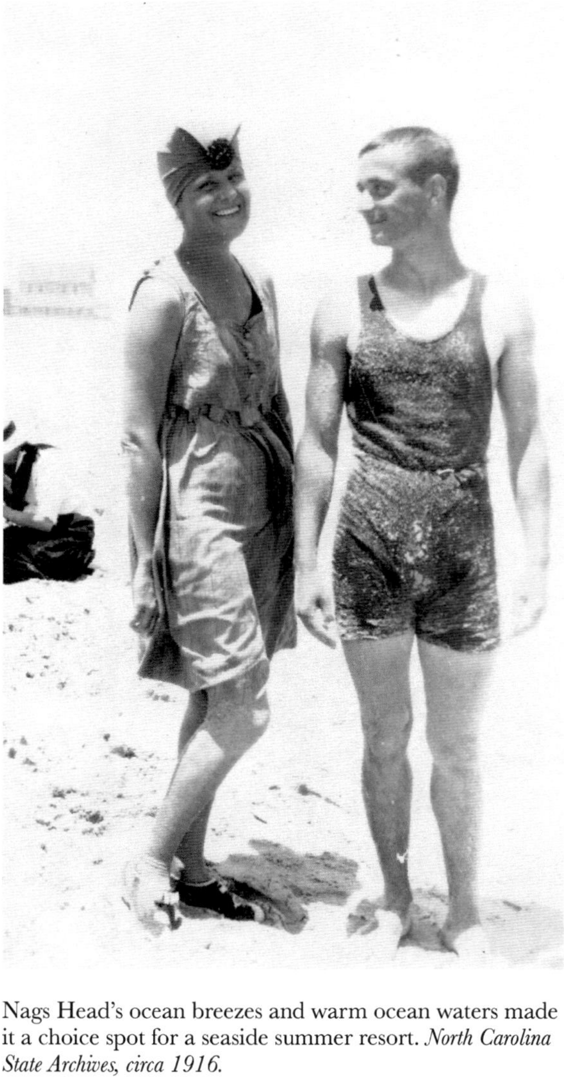

Nags Head's ocean breezes and warm ocean waters made it a choice spot for a seaside summer resort. *North Carolina State Archives, circa 1916.*

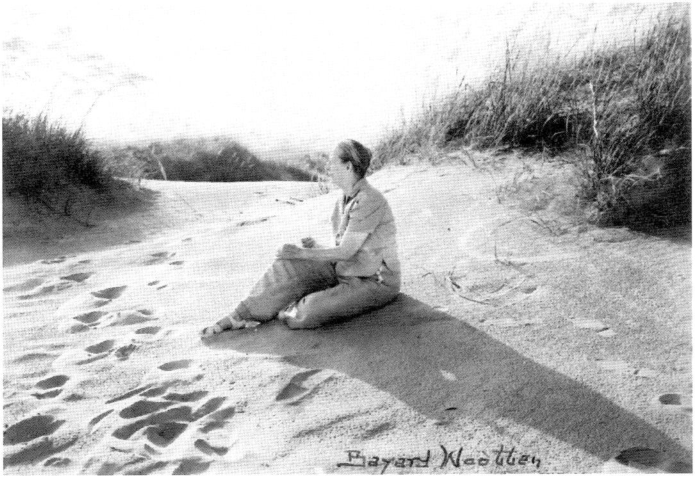


North Carolina photographer Bayard Wooten in the Nags Head dunes. Known for her landscape photography, Wooten photographed Jockey's Ridge. *North Carolina State Archives, circa 1925.*

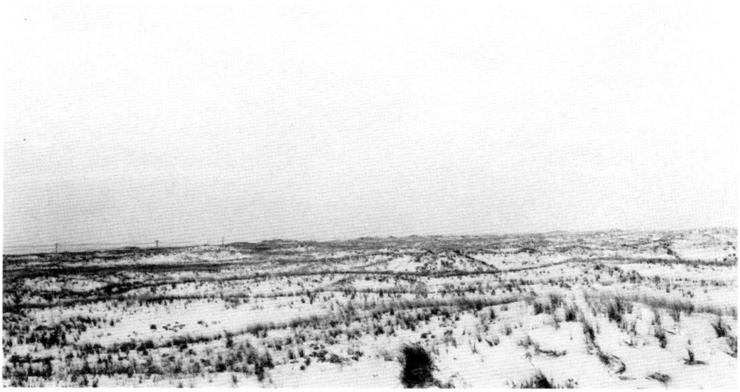

View south of Nags Head in the vicinity of Bodie Island. *North Carolina State Archives, 1926.*

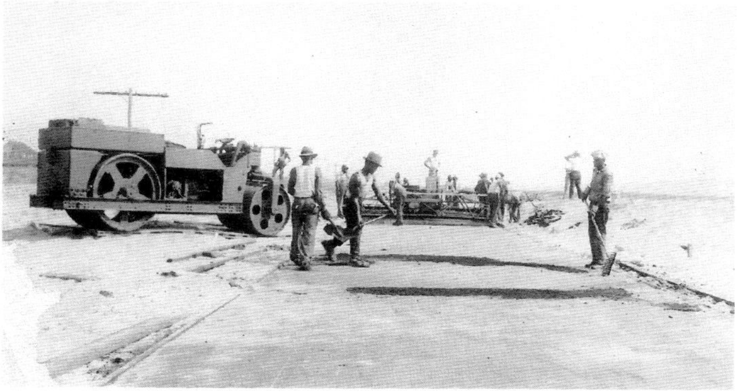

In the 1930s, the North Carolina General Assembly appropriated funds to build a road connecting the Wright Memorial Bridge, which spanned the Currituck Sound at Kitty Hawk, and the Roanoke Sound Bridge, which connected Roanoke Island and southern Nags Head. *Photo by D. Victor Meekins, Meekins Family Collection, Outer Banks History Center, circa 1931.*

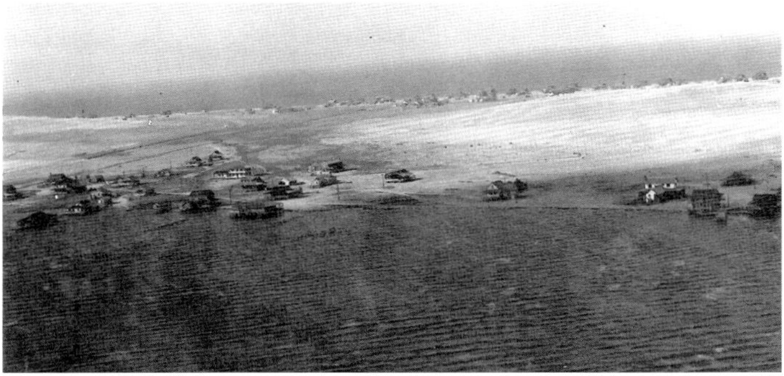

Aerial view of Nags Head showing both sound-side and oceanfront cottages. *Meekins Family Collection, Outer Banks History Center, circa 1935.*

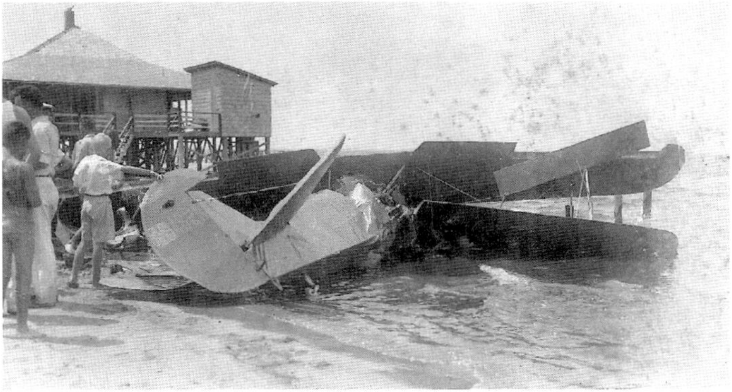

This fatal airplane crash on the sound side was used to urge Congress to designate funds for a planned airstrip at the Wright Brothers Memorial. According to the *Independent*, "For several years barnstorming pilots have been taking their planes to Nags Head during weekends in the summer and taking up passengers. All of these pilots have had to use unmarked sand flats for taking off and landing. With a fine landing field at Kill Devil Hill, just five miles north of Nags Head the sand flats would undoubtedly be abandoned." *David Stick Family Collection, Outer Banks History Center, 1936.*

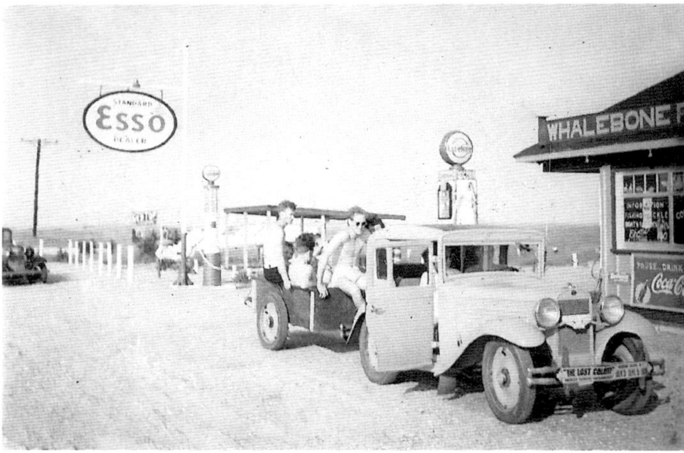


In the early 1930s, a Mr. Midgett opened a gas station at the southern end of Nags Head, where he displayed an old whale skeleton along with a sign suggesting that if drivers didn't purchase gas there, they would run out of fuel and dry up like the whale bones. That is how Whalebone Junction got its name. This image shows a group of *The Lost Colony* cast, choir and crew after a day on the beach. *Carolyn Horton Collection, Outer Banks History Center, circa 1948.*

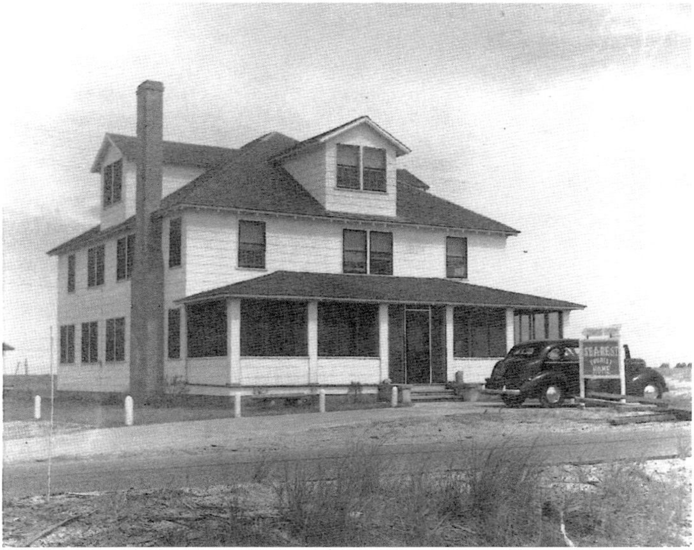

Leo and Elma Midgette owned and operated Sea Rest Tourist Home during the 1940s and 1950s. Its Whalebone Junction location made it convenient to fishing at Jennette's Pier and a short drive to Roanoke Island and *The Lost Colony* drama. *Courtesy Robert Midgette, circa 1950.*

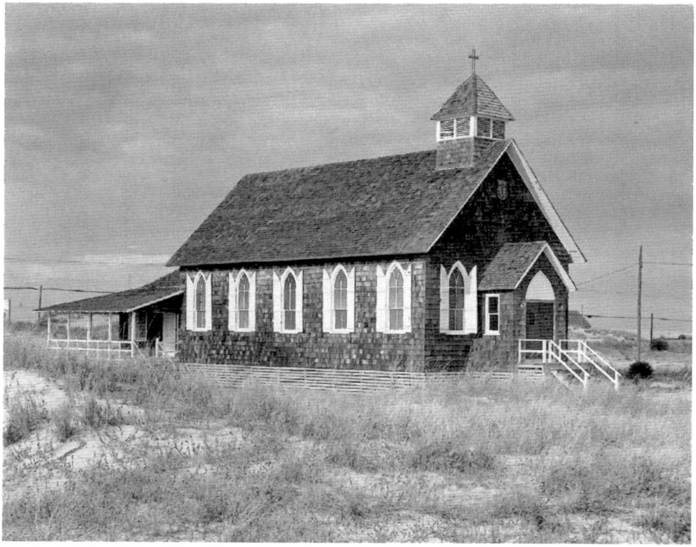

St. Andrew's by the Sea is the second Episcopal chapel to welcome worshipers in Nags Head. All Saints Chapel, constructed prior to the Civil War, was torn down by Federal troops who used its lumber at the Freedman's Colony on Roanoke Island. St. Andrew's was built by Stephen J. Twine in 1914 midway between the ocean and the sound. The chapel was moved to its present location in 1937. A larger sanctuary was completed in 2003, but the original chapel is still used for weddings, funerals and small services. *Photo by J. Foster Scott, Outer Banks History Center, 1971.*

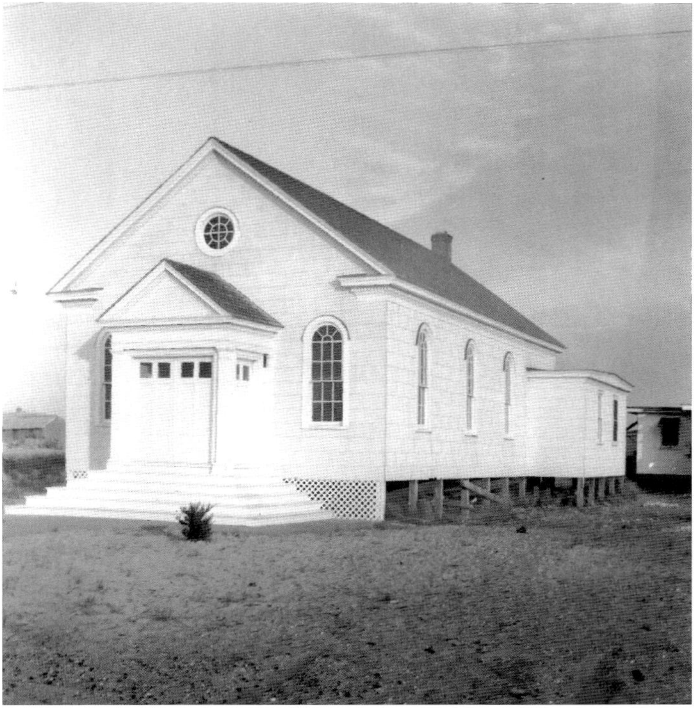

Nags Head Baptist Church was designed by Frank Dinwiddie, who in addition to being a preacher also worked as a carpenter, painter and fisherman. The 1,200-square-foot building was built by members of the Nags Head community and was ready for services in 1949. The first worshipers sat on pews made of fish crates and wooden planks. A new larger building, now known simply as Nags Head Church, was completed in 2007, and the original chapel was torn down. *Photo by Aycock Brown, Outer Banks History Center, 1958.*

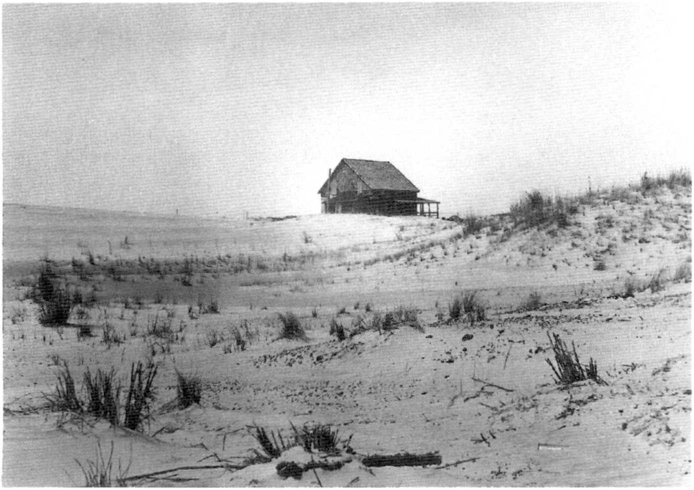

The H.V. Dunstan Cottage was moved near Jockey's Ridge after the Ash Wednesday Storm of 1962. It was one of the earliest oceanfront cottages, built in 1887, where it weathered storms for seventy-five years. It was razed in 2000. *Photo by Aycock Brown, Outer Banks History Center, circa 1970.*

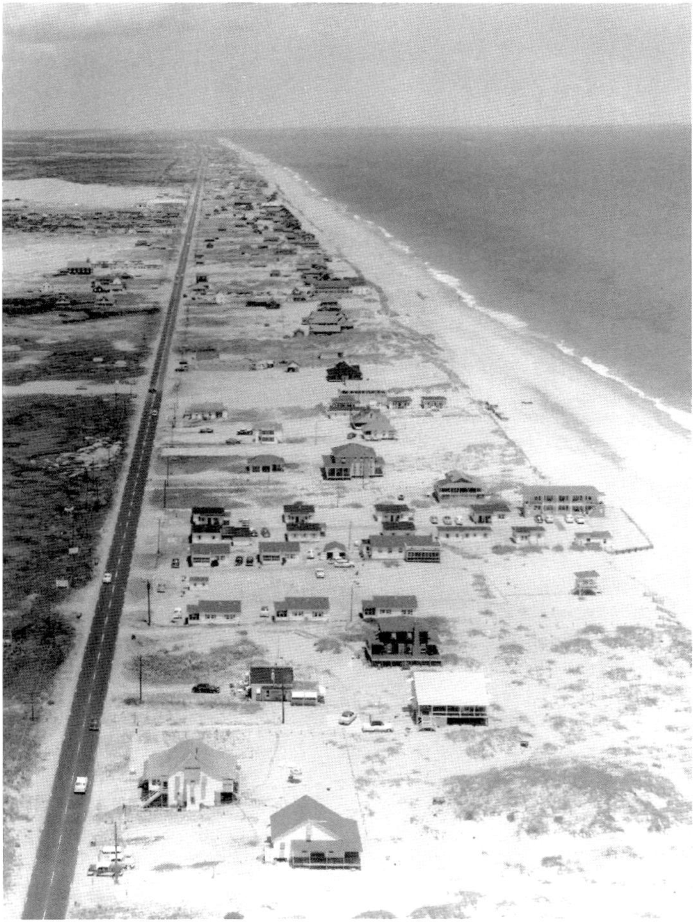

Aerial view of the Beach Road near milepost 13.5. *Photo by Aycock Brown, Outer Banks History Center, 1957.*

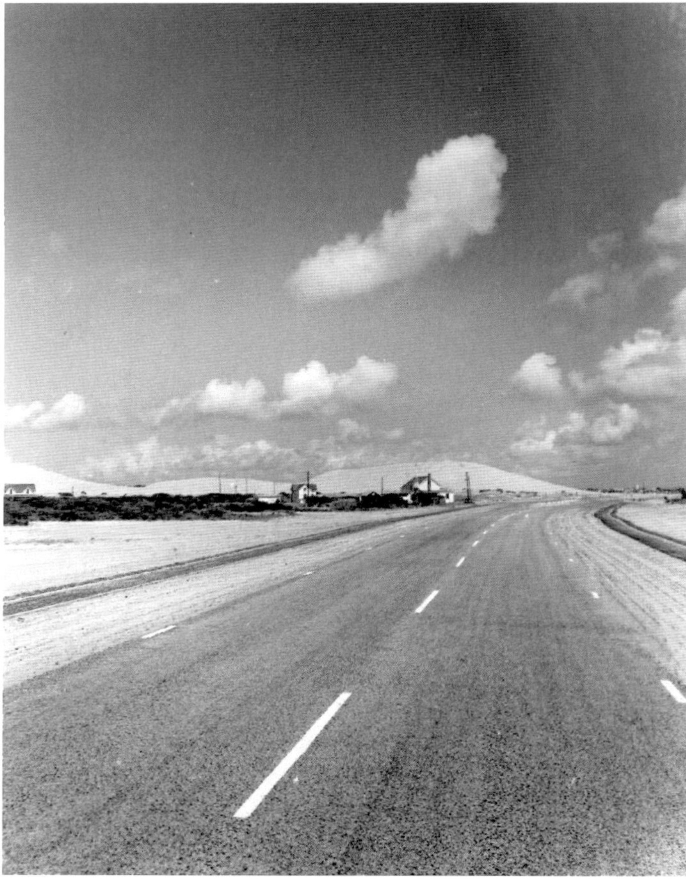

As the Outer Banks grew, a second thoroughfare was built parallel to and west of the Virginia Dare Trail. This U.S. 158 Bypass created additional road frontage for businesses. *Photo by Aycock Brown, Outer Banks History Center, 1959.*

Chapter 2

# JOCKEY'S RIDGE AND THE DUNES

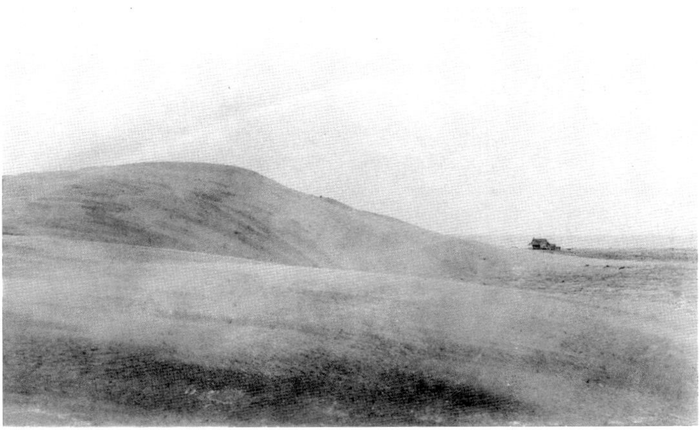

South of Jockey's Ridge was Engagement Hill, followed by the Seven Sisters. *North Carolina State Archives, 1911.*

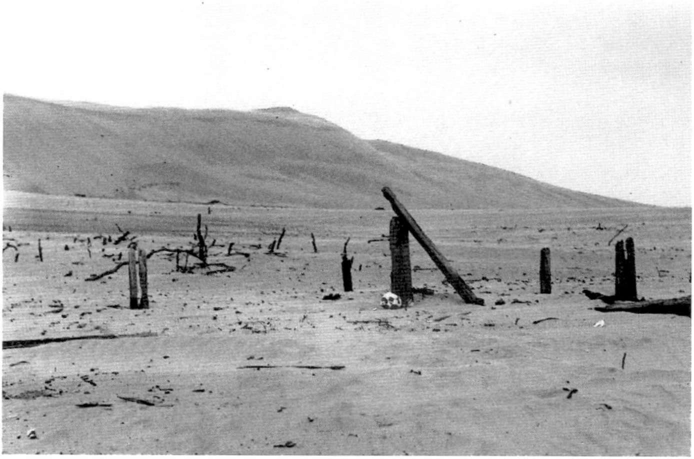

The Seven Sisters covered up this cemetery for a number of years until it was unearthed after a severe blow. *Photo by Bill Sharpe, Meekins Family Collection, Outer Banks History Center, circa 1950.*

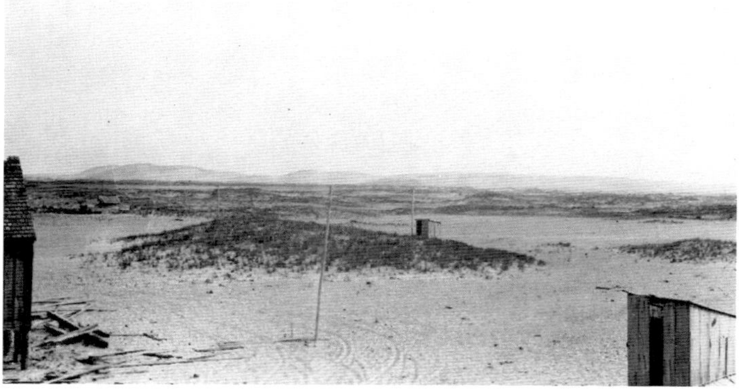

Nags Head's dunes stretched from Kill Devil Hill to Wreck Hill near Oregon Inlet. *North Carolina State Archives, 1911.*

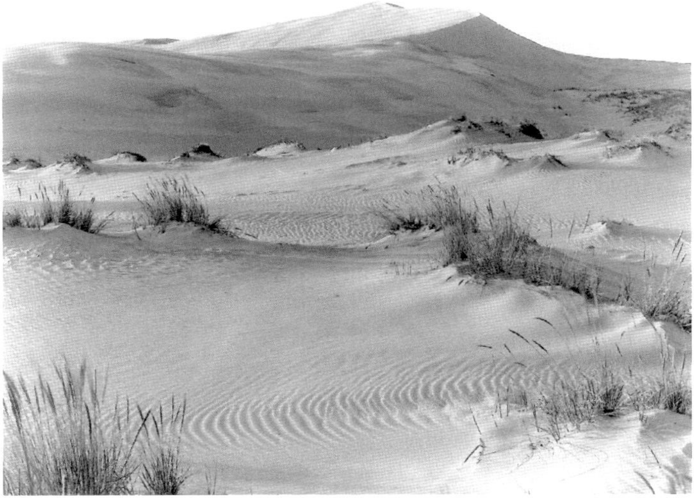

The ever-changing dunes of Jockey's Ridge. *Photo by J. Foster Scott, Outer Banks History, circa 1970.*

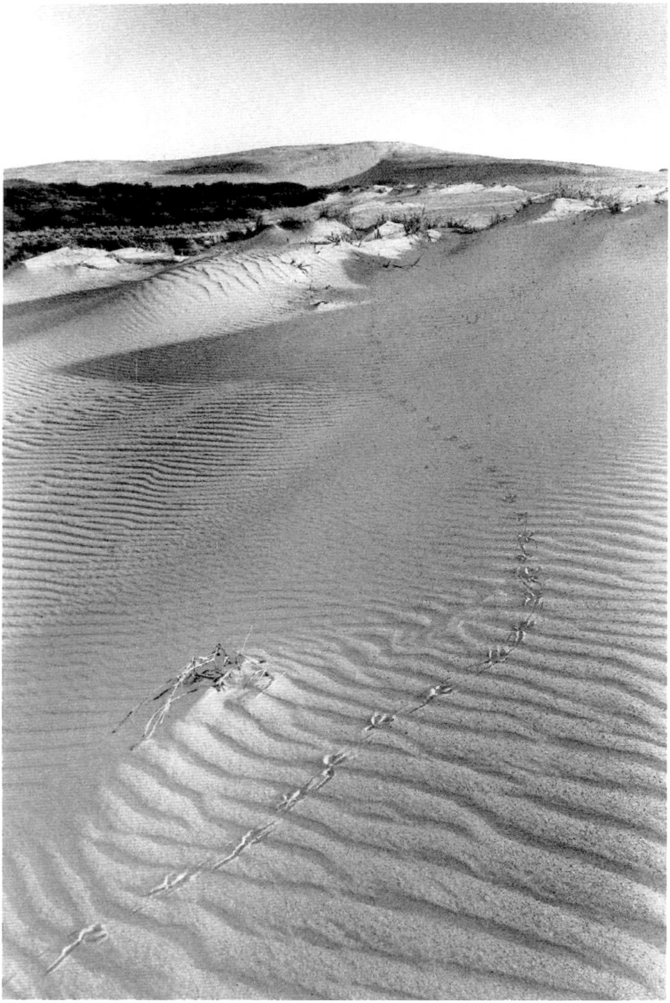

Tracks in the sand at Jockey's Ridge State Park. *Photo by Drew C. Wilson, Outer Banks History Center, circa 1990.*

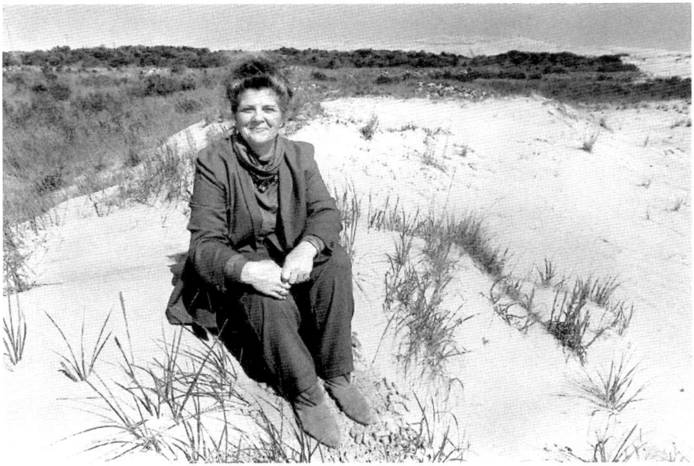

Carolista Fletcher Baum at Jockey's Ridge State Park. She was instrumental in preserving the Nags Head landmark. *Photo by Drew C. Wilson, Outer Banks History Center, 1990.*

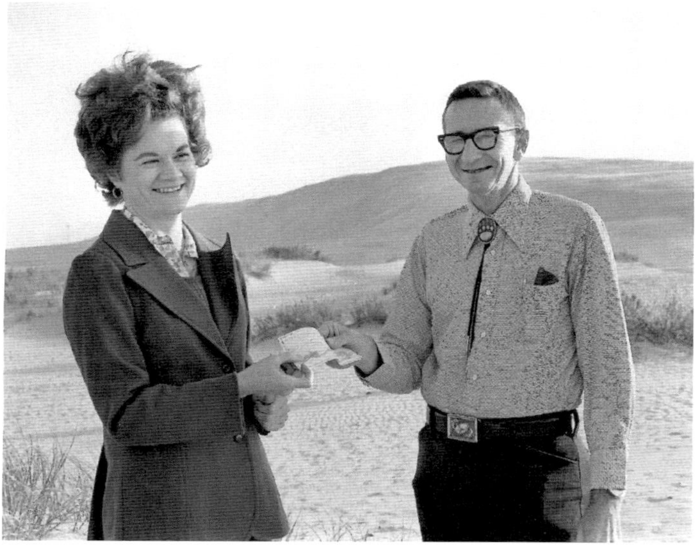

Marlene Roberts and Carl Nunemaker, who served on the board of directors of the People to Preserve Jockey's Ridge, in front of the dunes they helped to save. *Photo by J. Foster Scott, Outer Banks History Center, 1974.*

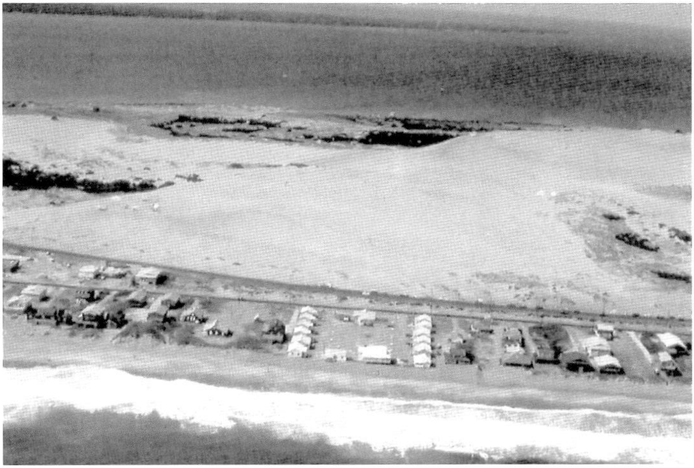

Aerial view of Jockey's Ridge State Park. *Photo by Jim Lee, 1978.*

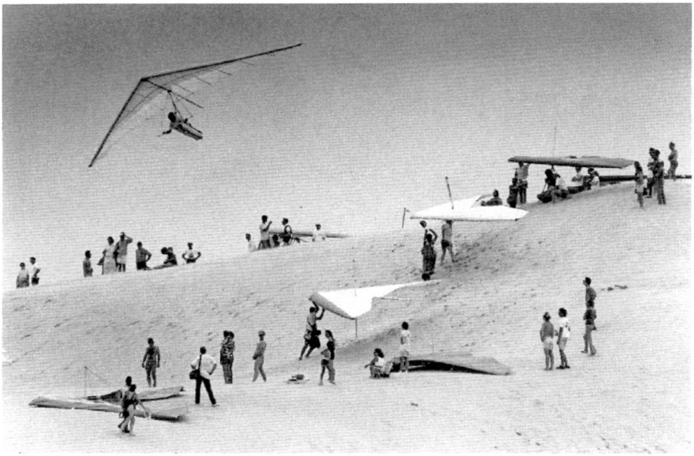

Hang gliders in the sixteenth annual Hang Gliding Spectacular at Jockey's Ridge State Park. The event, held each year since 1972, predates the state park. *Photo by Drew C. Wilson, Outer Banks History Center, 1988.*

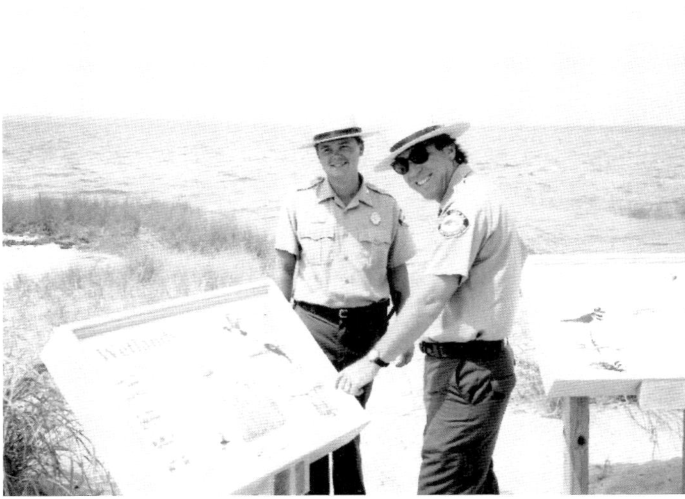

John Fullwood and George Barnes show off new interpretive signs at the sound-side beach that were provided by Carolina Light and Power and the North Carolina Coastal Federation in honor of the Year of the Coast. *Courtesy Jockey's Ridge State Park, 1994.*

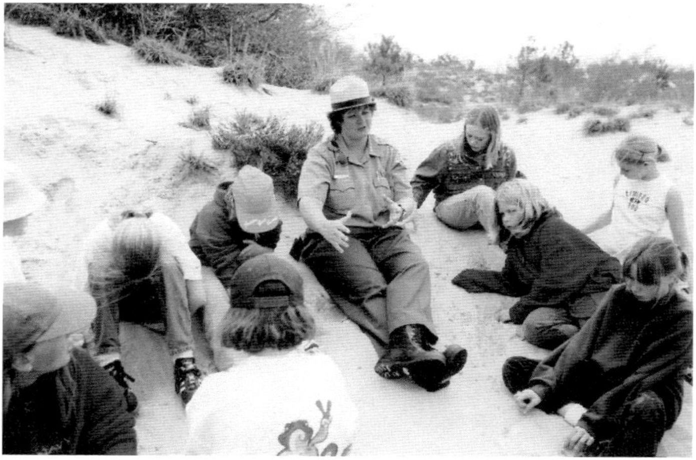

Ranger Kelley Thompson presents an environmental education program to a group of Girl Scouts. *Courtesy Jockey's Ridge State Park, circa 1997.*

# Chapter 3
# NAGS HEAD WOODS

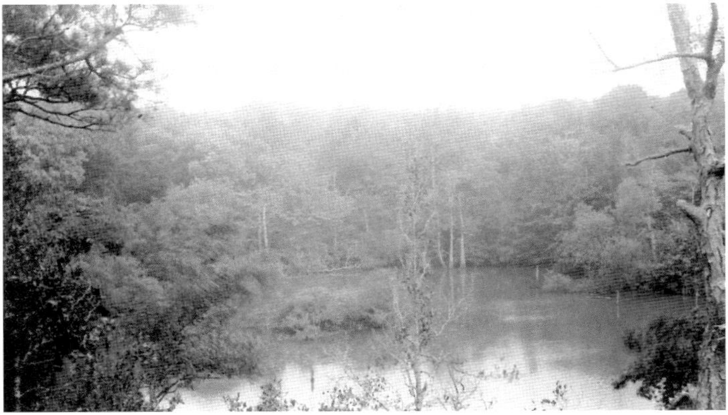

The protected maritime forest of Nags Head Woods is home to towering hardwoods, delicate flowers, freshwater ponds, birds, fish, mammals, reptiles and amphibians. Its unique makeup creates a diverse ecology found nowhere else in the world. *North Carolina State Archives, circa 1911.*

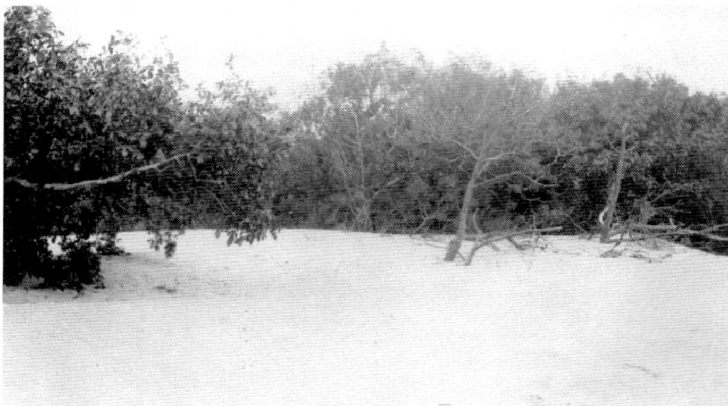

Nags Head Woods is shielded from the harsh Outer Banks environment by a series of dunes and ridges. *North Carolina State Archives, circa 1920.*

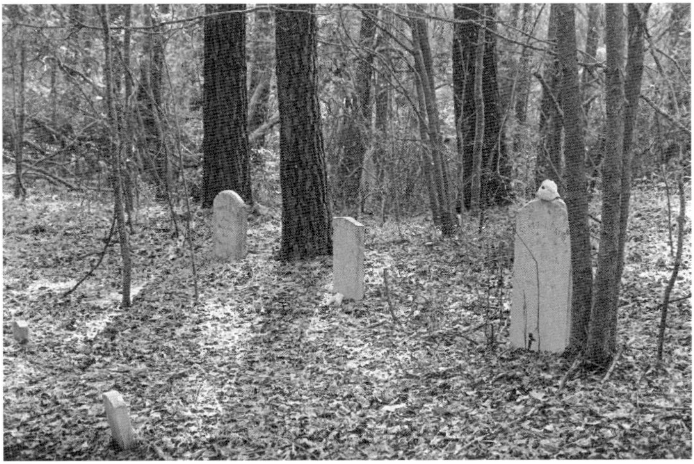

By the early nineteenth century, "bankers" were living in Nags Head Woods. Some early surnames of woods dwellers are Mann, Partridge, Baum, Twiford, Tillett, Toler, Beasley, O'Neal and Peterson. *Photo by J. Foster Scott, courtesy TNC, Nags Head Woods Preserve Photo Archive, circa 1970.*

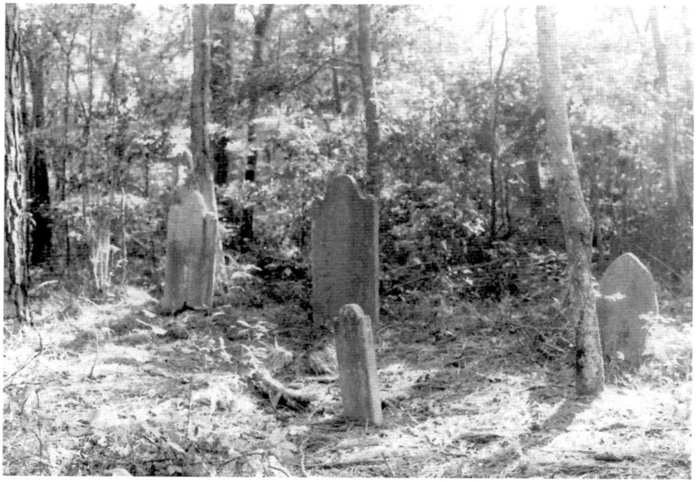

Little remains of the settlement in Nags Head Woods other than family cemeteries. The community was once large enough to support two churches and a school. An 1893 census reflected forty-five students attending the wood-frame schoolhouse. It closed in the early 1930s. *Courtesy TNC, Nags Head Woods Preserve Photo Archive, date unknown.*

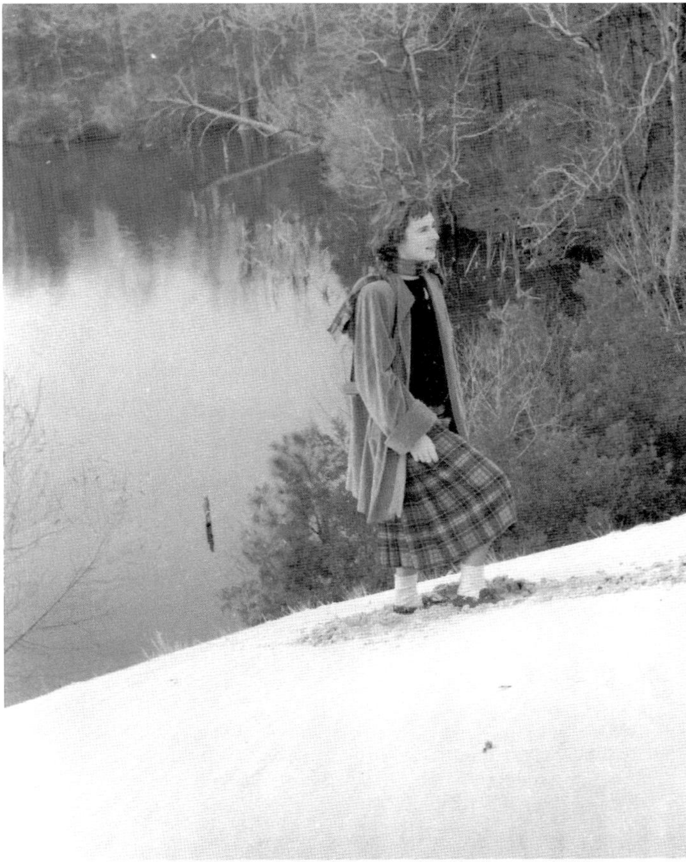

Elevations in Nags Head Woods range from zero to seventy feet above sea level. *Photo by Aycock Brown, Outer Banks History Center, 1950s.*

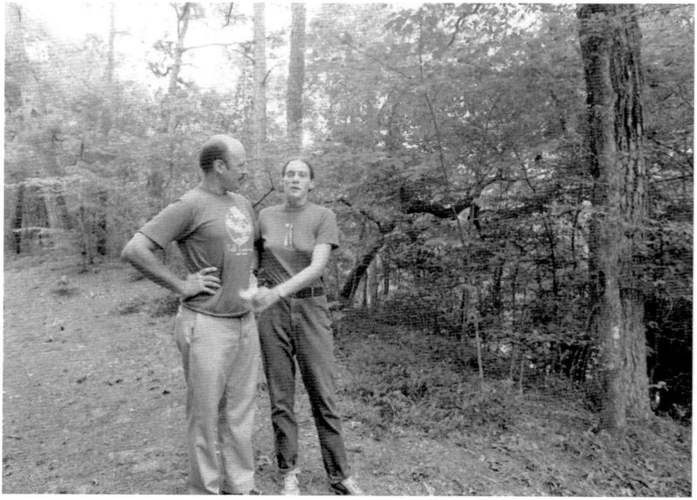

Jim and Henrietta List were the first director and steward of Nags Head Woods Ecological Preserve, serving from its inception until 1988. *Courtesy TNC, Nags Head Woods Preserve Photo Archive, circa 1980.*

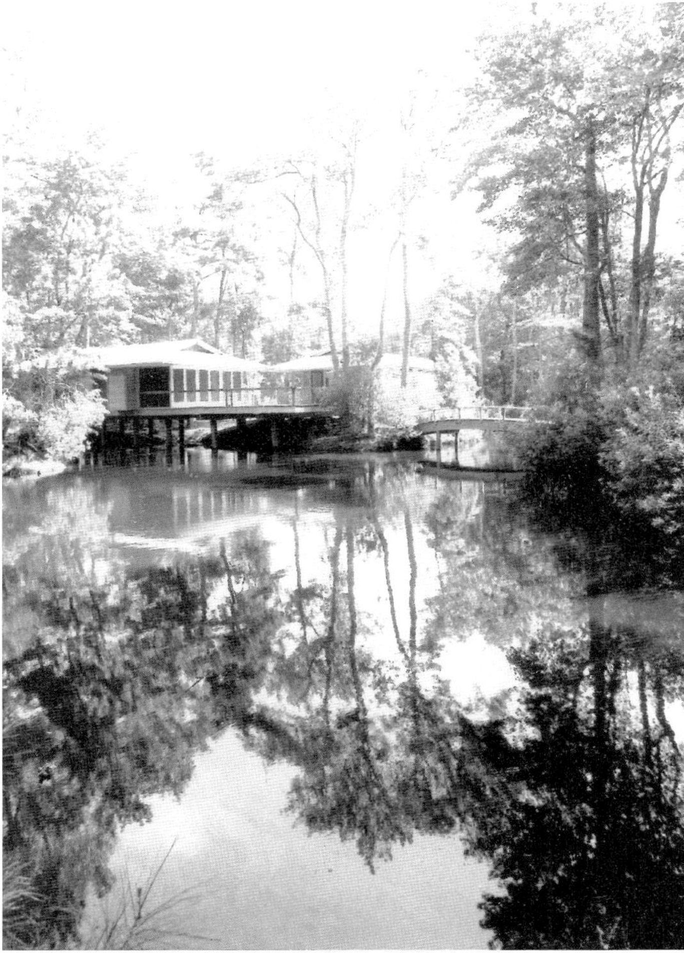

The Visitor Center at Nags Head Woods was dedicated in 1984 and was later named for Gordon Hayes, one of the woods' early benefactors. *Photo by Rich Beckman, courtesy TNC, Nags Head Woods Preserve Photo Archive, circa 1984.*

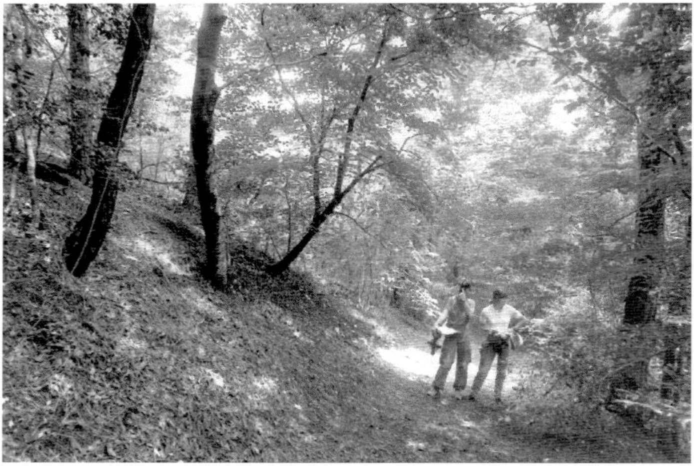

Scientists Sharon LaPalme and Cindy Gill discuss placement of a test plot used to determine long-term changes within the ecosystem. Nags Head Woods' unique collection of flora and fauna make it a living classroom for students of botany, biology, forestry and coastal ecology. *Photo by Drew C. Wilson, Outer Banks History Center, 1990.*

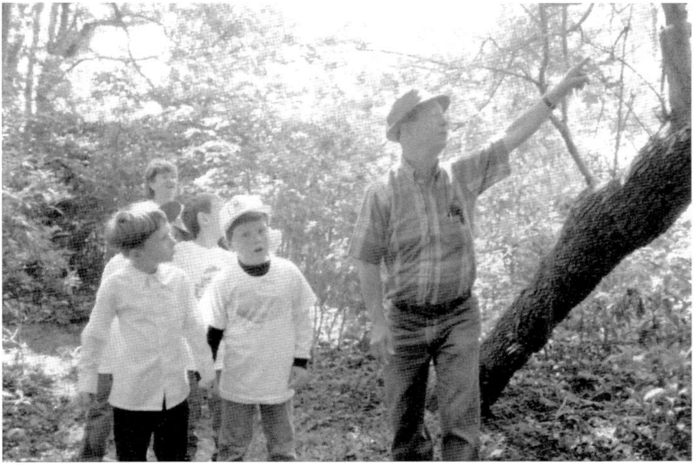

Nags Head Woods sponsored summer eco-camps to introduce children to the maritime forest environment. Dave Leake leads a nature walk. *Photo by Jeff Smith DeBlieu, courtesy TNC, Nags Head Woods Preserve Photo Archive, circa 1996.*

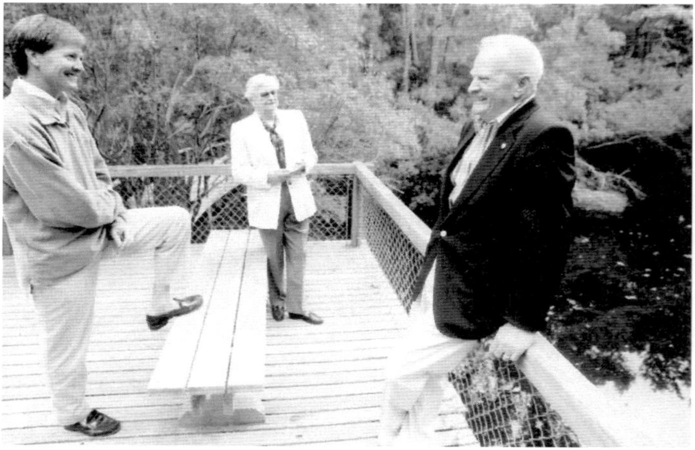

Jeff Smith DeBlieu, Kay Bryan and Don Bryan on the deck of the Visitor Center. DeBlieu was director at Nags Head Woods from 1988 to 2005. The Bryans have been active supporters of the woods, serving on the Friends of Nags Head Woods Board of Directors and providing financial aid. Don served as a Nags Head commissioner and mayor from 1975 to 1991 and helped to ensure that the woods would be preserved. *Photo by Drew C. Wilson, courtesy TNC, Nags Head Woods Preserve Photo Archive, 1998.*

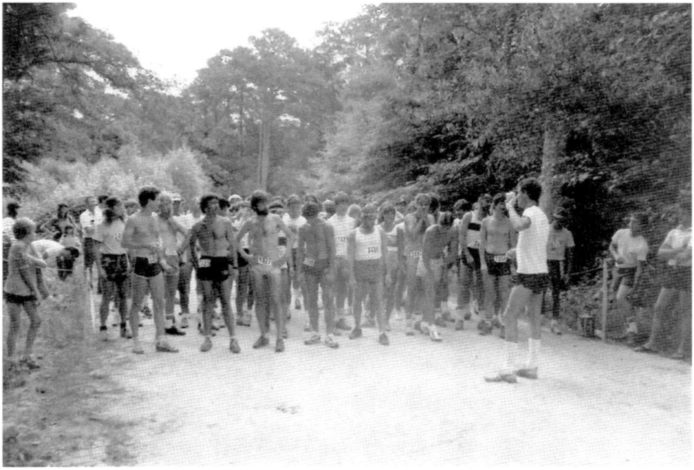

The Nags Head Woods Run has been an established event for over twenty-five years. The five-kilometer race runs through the maritime forest. Larry Gray briefs participants in the first Nags Head Woods Run. *Courtesy TNC, Nags Head Woods Preserve Photo Archive, 1984.*

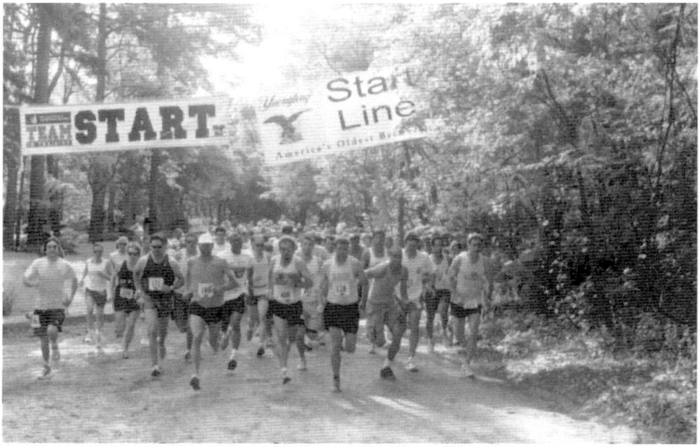


Runners in the annual Nags Head Woods 5K Run. The event draws hundreds of participants from North Carolina, Virginia and the mid-Atlantic States. *Photo by Lisa Loy, 2004.*

# Chapter 4
# U.S. LIFE-SAVING SERVICE AND U.S. COAST GUARD

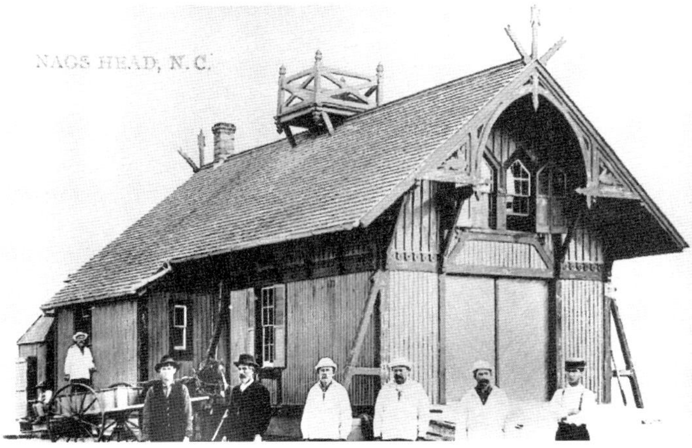


Seven lifesaving stations were built on the Outer Banks in 1874, known as "1874-type" stations. A blend of carpenter gothic and stick-style architecture, they featured elaborate exterior trim. The Nags Head Station was built one and a half miles south of the Nags Head resort and seven and a half miles north of Bodie Island Lighthouse. Other stations of this type were Chicamacomico, Kitty Hawk, Little Kinnakeet, Bodie Island, Caffey's Inlet and Currituck Beach. John W. Evans, M.W. Etheridge, B.F. Meekins, Van Buren Etheridge and Eugene H. Peel were early keepers at the station. *Courtesy National Park Service, circa 1880.*

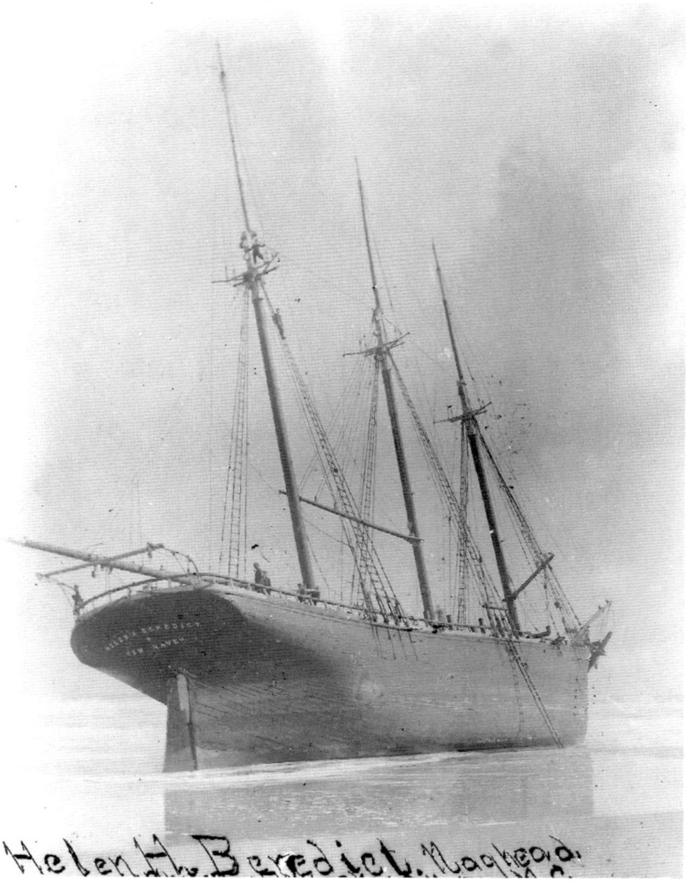


The *Helen H. Benedict* ran aground in thick, foggy weather at Nags Head en route from Perth Amboy, New Jersey, to Fernandina Beach, Florida. *Photo by D. Victor Meekins, Outer Banks History Center, 1914.*

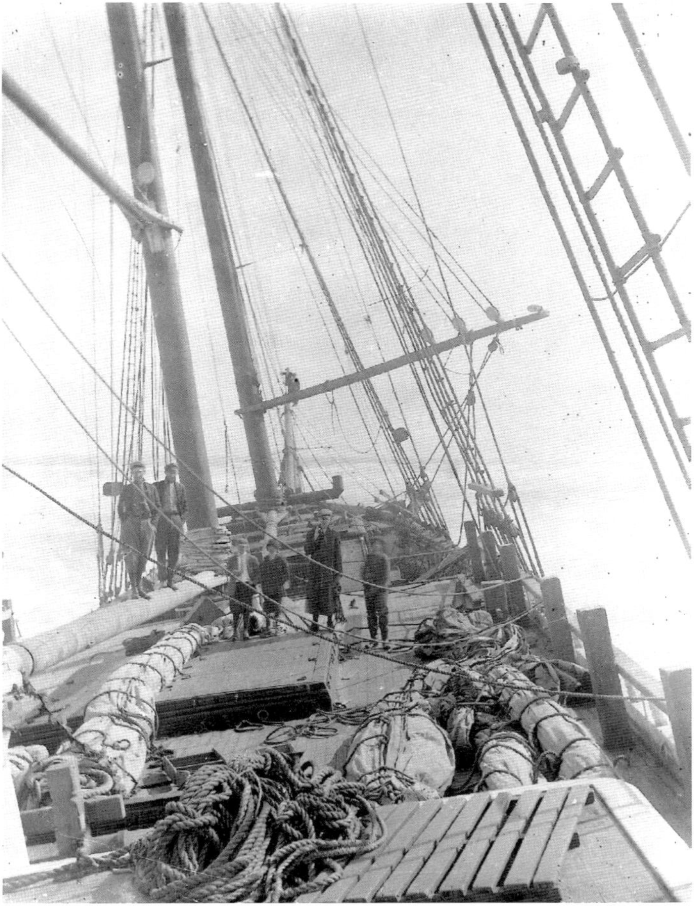

View of the deck of the *Helen H. Benedict*. The captain and crew of six were rescued by the men of the Nags Head Life-saving Station. *Photo by D. Victor Meekins, Outer Banks History Center, 1914.*

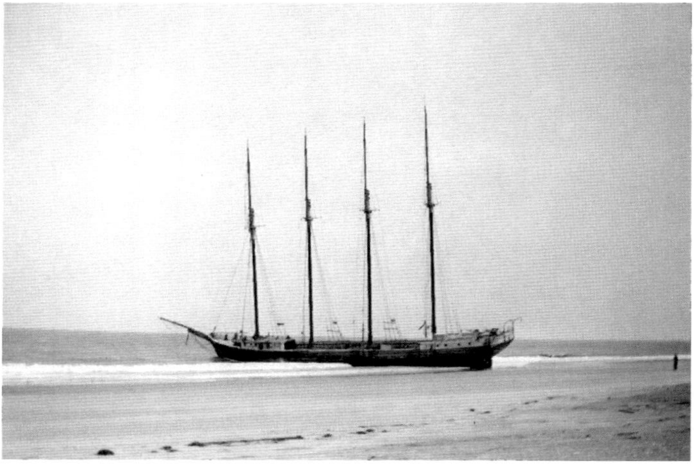

The *Bainbridge* was carrying a load of rough lumber when it sailed from Jacksonville, Florida, bound for Fair Haven, Massachusetts. The crew was rescued by a group of Coast Guardsmen under the direction of Herman C. Smith of the Bodie Island Station after the schooner went ashore a mile south of the Nags Head Station. *Courtesy the Mariners' Museum, Newport News, Virginia, 1929.*

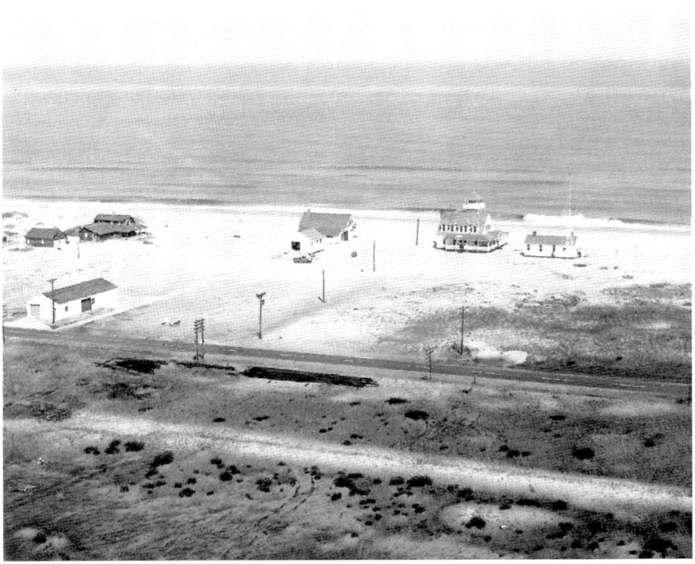

A second lifesaving station was built in Nags Head in 1912 and was known as a "Chicamacomico-type" station. To the right of the main building is the kitchen and to the immediate left is the boathouse and garage. As one of the only buildings in Nags Head with a telephone, it was a center of communications. *National Archives photo no. 26-LB-Q-1, 1954.*

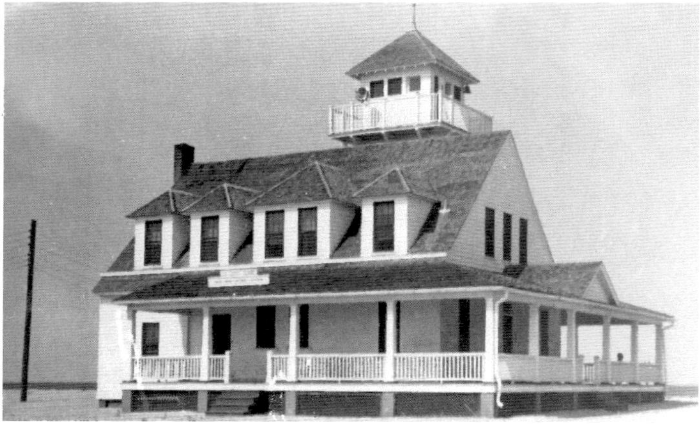

Chicamacomico-type stations featured a gable roof, hip dormers, a hipped roof watchtower and a wide porch on two sides. In 1915, the U.S. Coast Guard was created when the U.S. Life-saving Service and the U.S. Revenue Cutter Service merged. The station was then known as the Nags Head Coast Guard Station. *Courtesy National Park Service, 1954.*

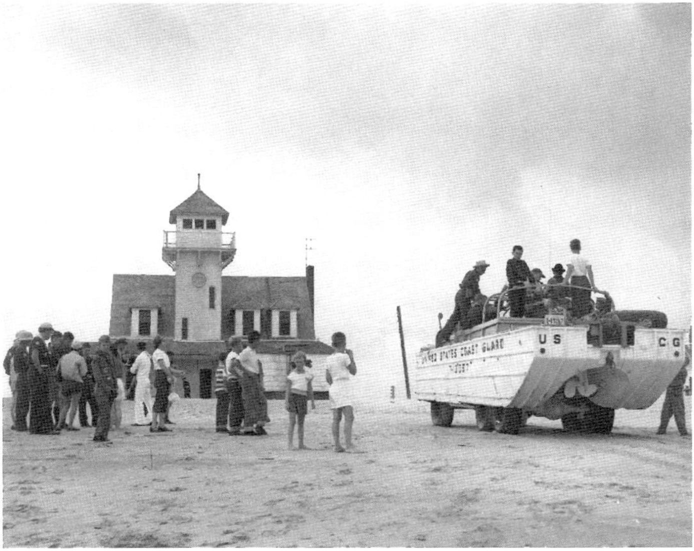


Boy Scouts visiting the Nags Head Coast Guard Station get a close-up look at a DUKW, an amphibious vehicle commonly referred to as a "duck." DUKWs were used by the army to transport troops during World War II. Following the war, the Coast Guard modified the DUKWs, which were used for rescues, especially during floods. *Courtesy National Park Service, circa 1958.*

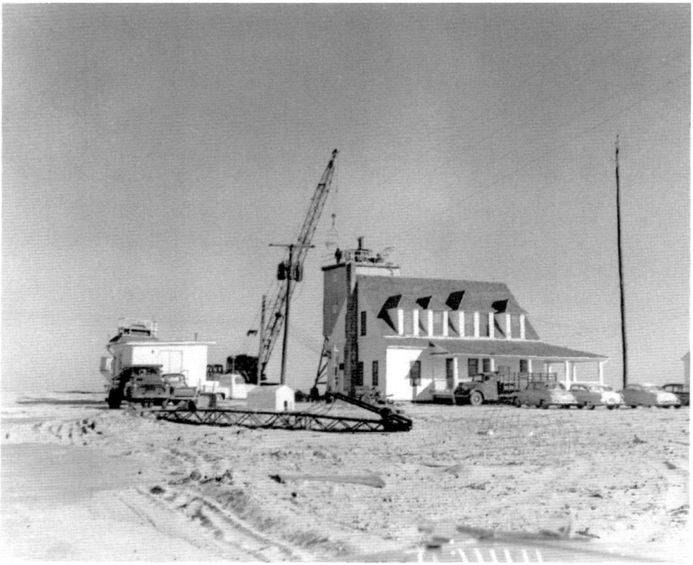

The Nags Head Coast Guard Station was turned over to the General Services Administration in 1957 and transferred to the Department of the Army in 1961, when it became an army radar station shortly before it was severely damaged the following year in the Ash Wednesday Storm. The radar tower is under construction. *Photo by Aycock Brown, Outer Banks History Center, circa 1960.*

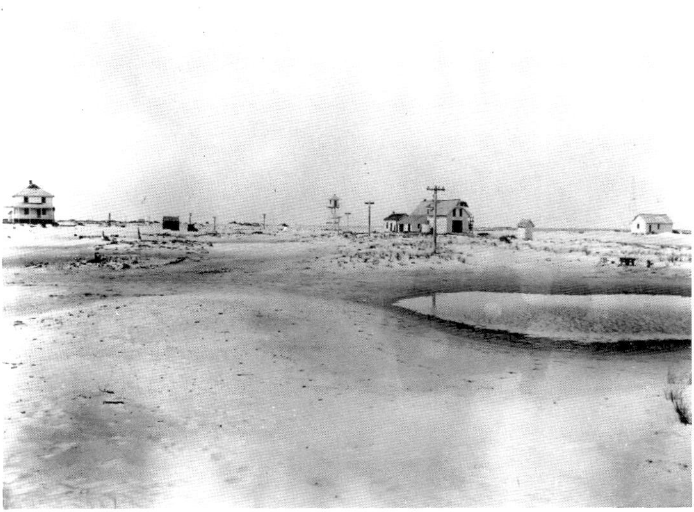

Tommy's Hummock Life-saving Station was built in 1876 just over a mile northeast of Bodie Island Lighthouse. It was named Bodie Island Station in 1883, and the former Bodie Island Station, south of Oregon Inlet, was named Oregon Inlet Station. A new building was constructed in 1923, known as a "Chatham-type" station. Both the original Tommy's Hummock Station and the 1923 Bodie Island Station are still standing and are listed on the National Register of Historic Places. *Courtesy Outer Banks History Center, date unknown.*

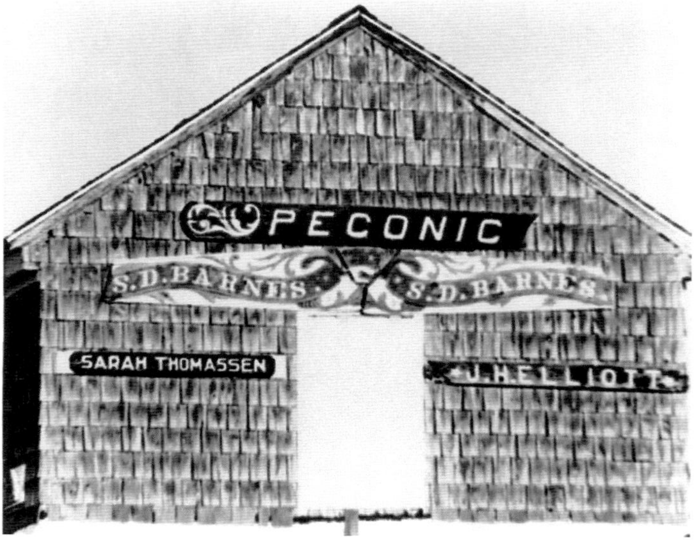


The Fearing Cottage on Nags Head's sound side was adorned with ships' side plates collected over many years. *Courtesy National Park Service, 1973.*

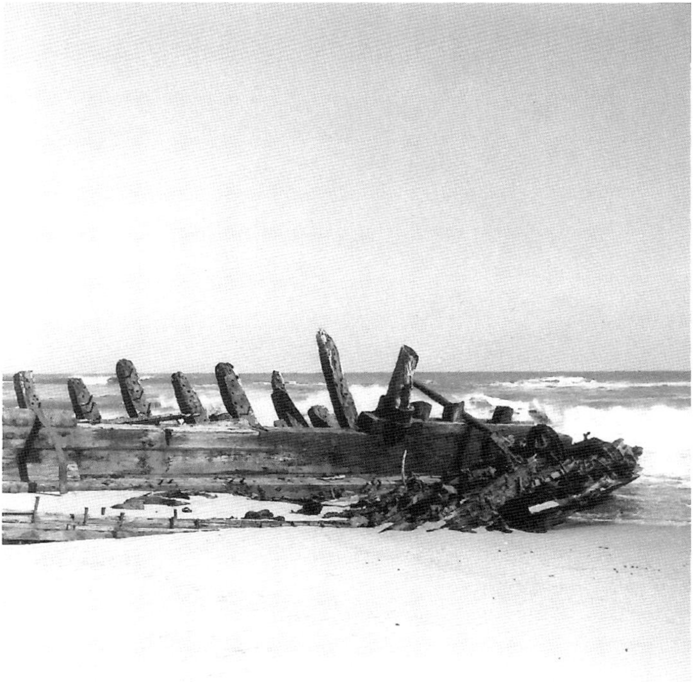

Remains of the three-masted schooner *Laura A. Barnes* that wrecked off Nags Head in 1921. *Photo by Aycock Brown, Outer Banks History Center, 1958.*

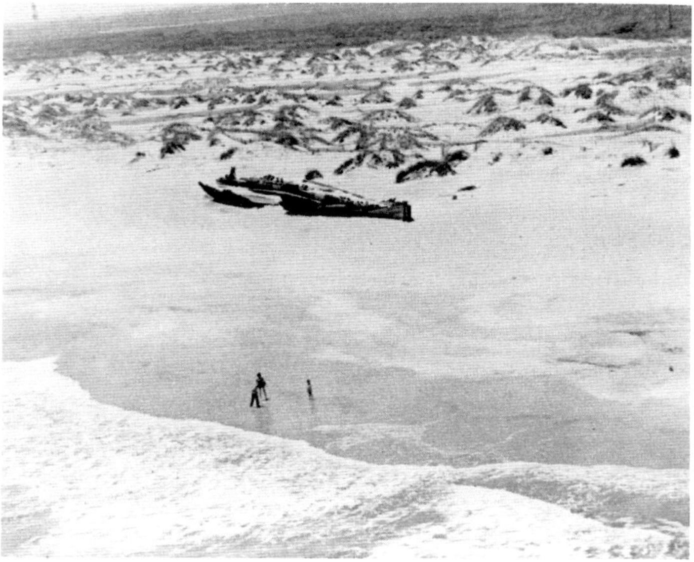

Aerial view of the wreck *Laura A. Barnes* near Coquina Beach. The Bodie Island Lighthouse is visible in the background. *Courtesy National Park Service, date unknown.*

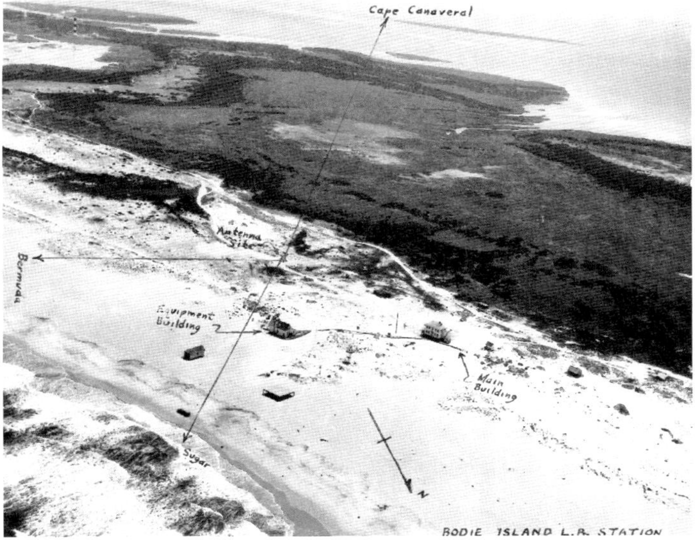


With the threat of war in the early 1940s, the United States worked on developing a reliable radio navigation system. Loran, short for Long Range Aid to Navigation, used a series of transmitters located along the coast, which sent out radio pulses. By reading the pulses from two transmitters, it was possible to determine a ship's location. The Bodie Island Coast Guard Station was used as a Loran Station from 1944 to 1949. *U.S. Coast Guard photo courtesy National Park Service, 1944.*

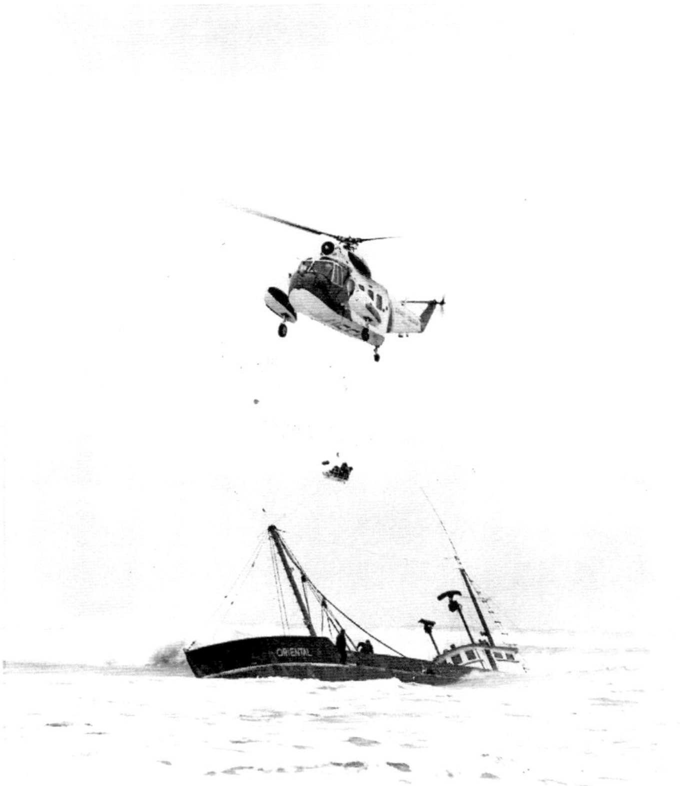


The trawler *Oriental* encountered foul weather and tried to enter Oregon Inlet when it struck ground near Bodie Island. A helicopter from Coast Guard Air Station Elizabeth City was quick to respond and rescued the captain and a crew of two via a life basket. United Press International named this image news photo of the month. *Photo by Aycock Brown, Outer Banks History Center, 1969.*

# Chapter 5
# OUR FISHING CULTURE

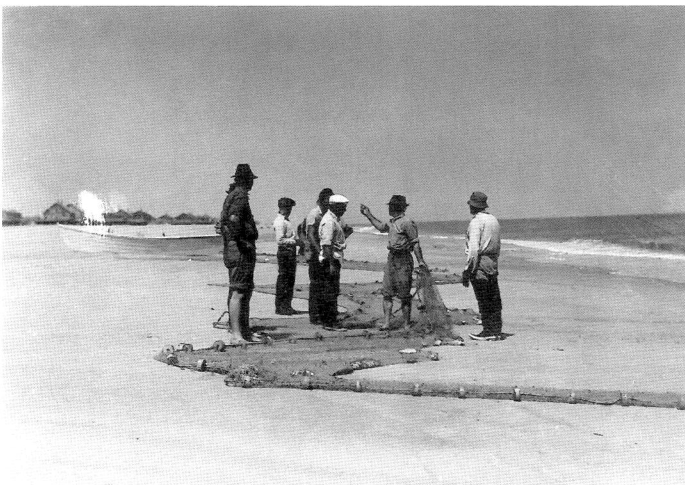

Fishermen at Nags Head. *Meekins Family Collection, Outer Banks History Center, circa 1935.*

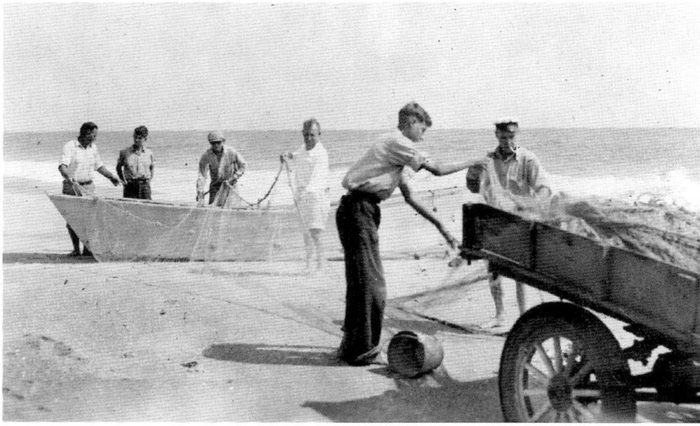

Fishing provided Nags Headers with sustenance and a commodity to trade or sell. *North Carolina Collection, University of North Carolina at Chapel Hill, 1938.*

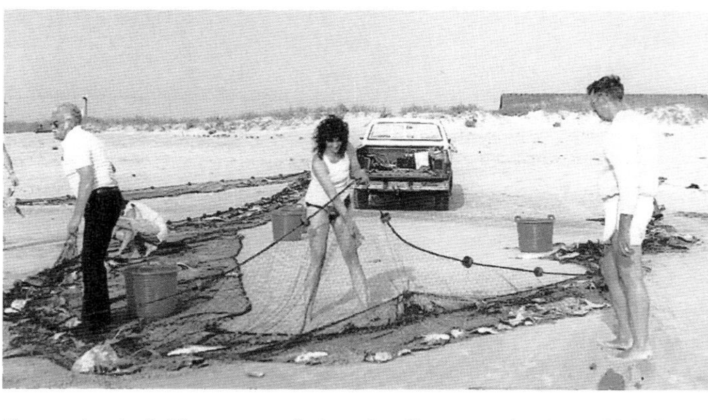

Jimmy Austin (left) gets some help unloading nets. Austin and his family have owned and operated Austin's Seafood across from Jockey's Ridge for over thirty years. *Courtesy Austin's Seafood, circa 1984.*

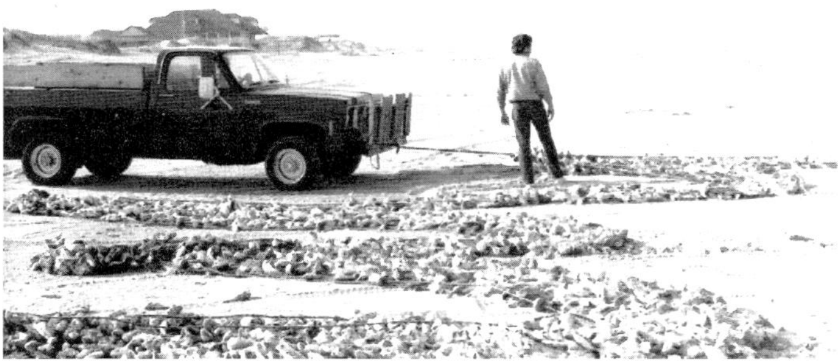

A haul of croakers made in two hours in early September. *Courtesy Budgie Sadler, circa 1980.*

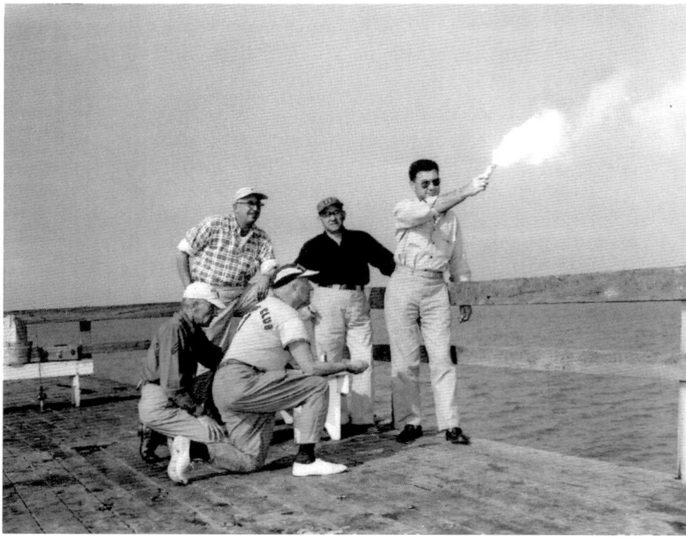


A flare was used to signal the start of the Nags Head Surf Fishing Tournament. *Photo by Aycock Brown, Outer Banks History Center, circa 1953.*

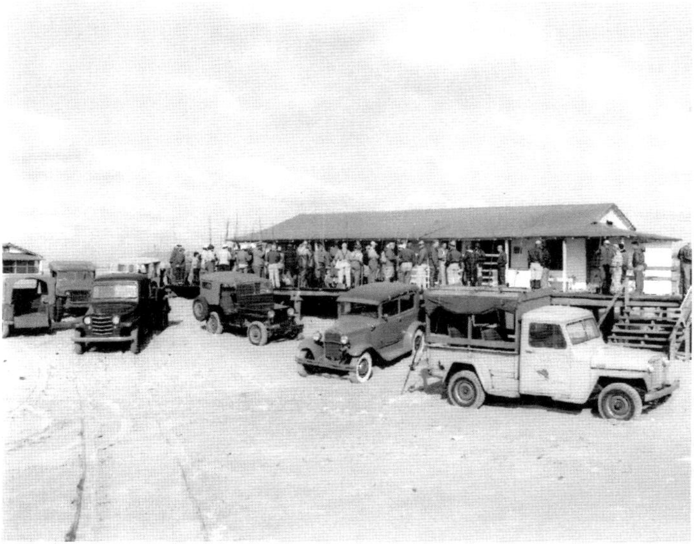

Jennette's Pier served as headquarters for the Nags Head Surf Fishing Tournament during its early years. *Photo by Aycock Brown, Outer Banks History Center, circa 1952.*

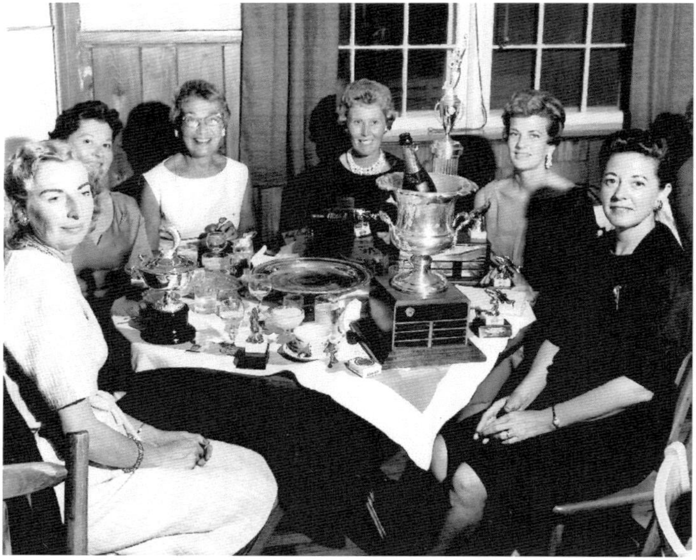

The North Carolina Sea Hags fishing team after winning the Harold Williams Trophy. They were the overall winners of the Nags Head Surf Fishing Tournament in 1965. *From left to right*: Elnora Preston, Claire Bullington, Texine Britt, Virginia Smith, Joyce Gunter and Margaret Sykes. *Photo by Aycock Brown, Outer Banks History Center, 1963.*

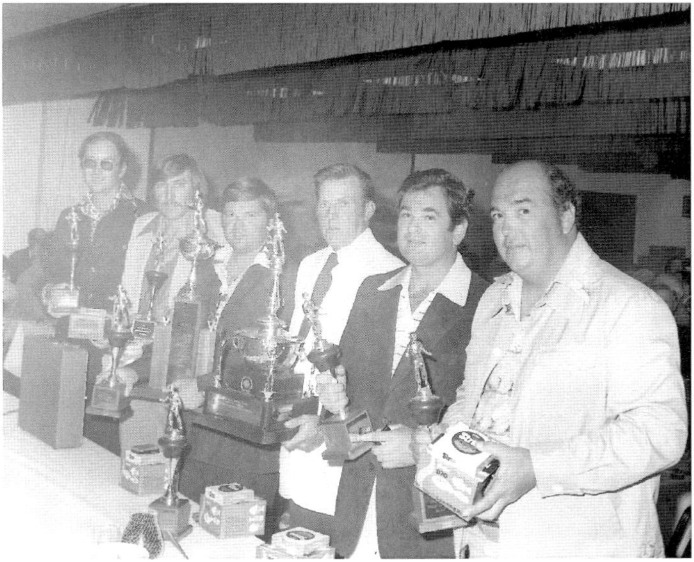

The Outer Banks Hurricanes (left to right), Jerry Wright, Rudy Gray, Sam Stokes, Dennis Midgett, Joe Martone and Lance Newman, at a Nags Head Surf Fishing Tournament awards ceremony. *Photo by Aycock Brown, Outer Banks History Center, circa 1976.*

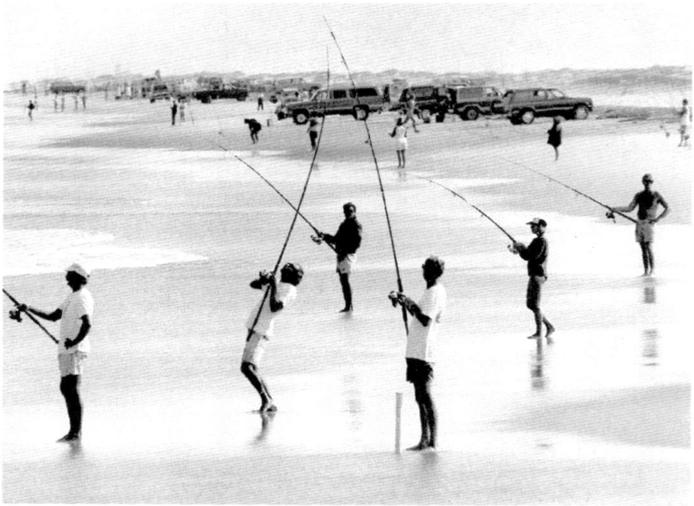

Members of the Rising Tides fishing team from Nags Head at Oregon Inlet during the forty-first Nags Head Surf Fishing Tournament. *Photo by Drew C. Wilson, Outer Banks History Center, 1991.*

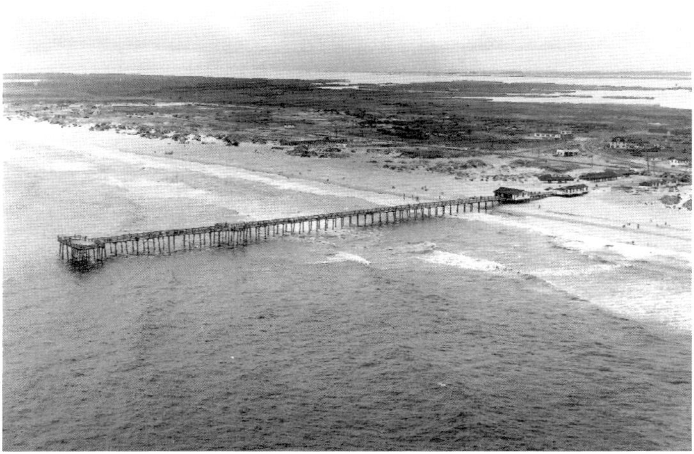

Jennette's Pier, built by Warren Jennette in 1939, was the first fishing pier in Nags Head and along the Outer Banks. It measured over 750 feet. The Virginia Dare Construction and Salvage Company was hired to do the work. The site of the pier was a former WPA transient labor camp. Some of the old camp buildings were refurbished and made into overnight accommodations. *Photo by Roger P. Meekins, Outer Banks History Center, circa 1954.*

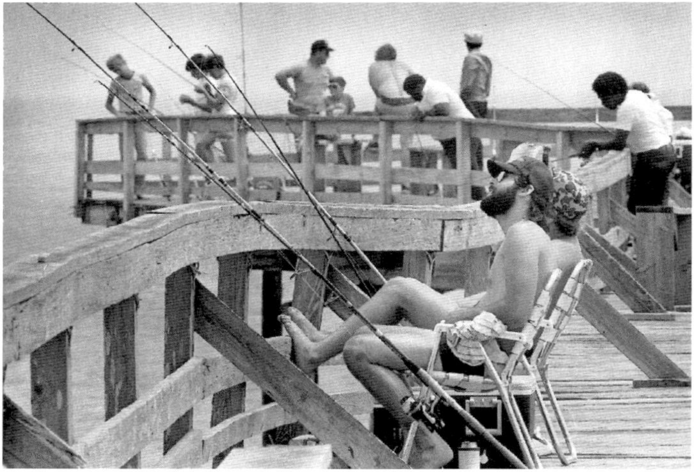

Waiting for a bite on Jennette's Pier. The pier was a victim of Hurricane Isabel in 2003, but it is soon to be rebuilt and administered by the North Carolina Aquarium Society. *Photo by Drew C. Wilson, Outer Banks History Center, 1986.*

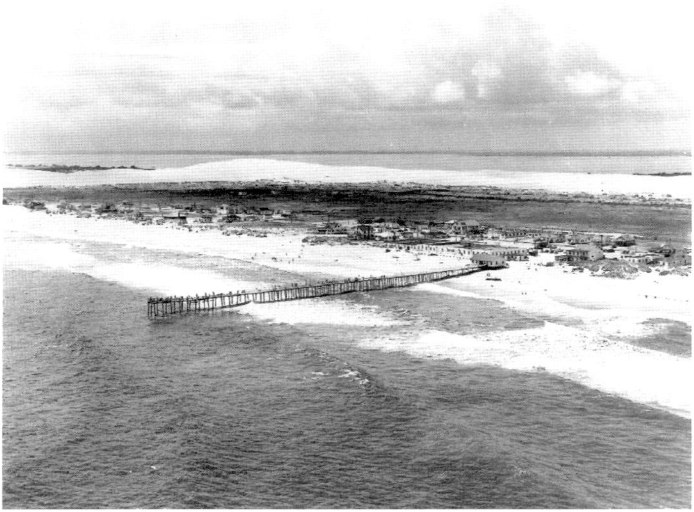

Mann's Ocean Pier was built in 1947 by Gaston Mann, who did much of the work himself. Now known as Nags Head Fishing Pier, it continues to attract anglers each year. *Photo by Roger P. Meekins, Outer Banks History Center, circa 1954.*

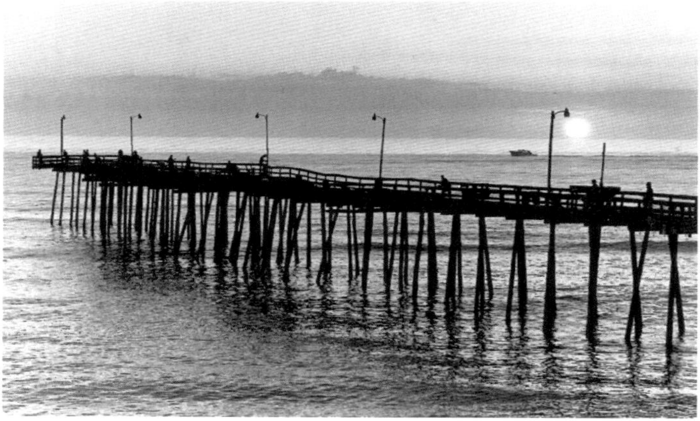

West Virginia native Red Mitchell built the Seaport Pier in South Nags Head in the late 1950s. It is known today as Outer Banks Pier. *Photo by Drew C. Wilson, Outer Banks History Center, circa 1990.*

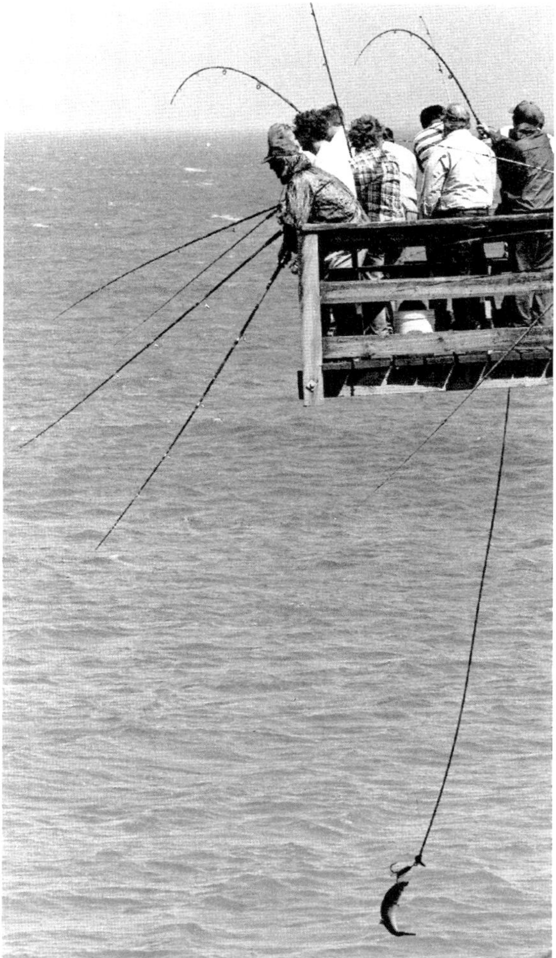

Anglers crowd the north corner of the Outer Banks Pier during a bluefish blitz. *Photo by Drew C. Wilson, Outer Banks History Center, circa 1990.*

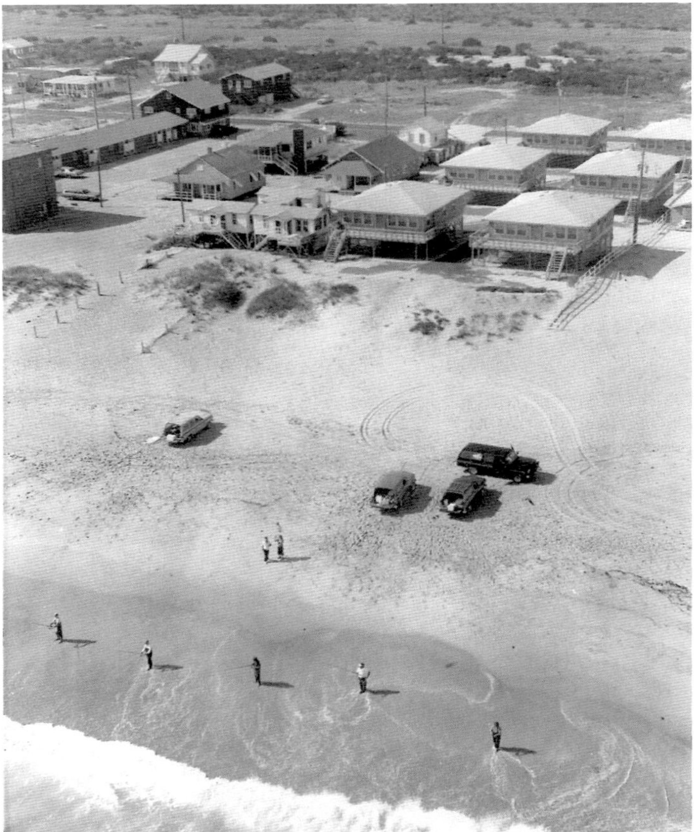

Surf fishing near milepost 16. *Photo by Aycock Brown, Outer Banks History Center, circa 1960.*

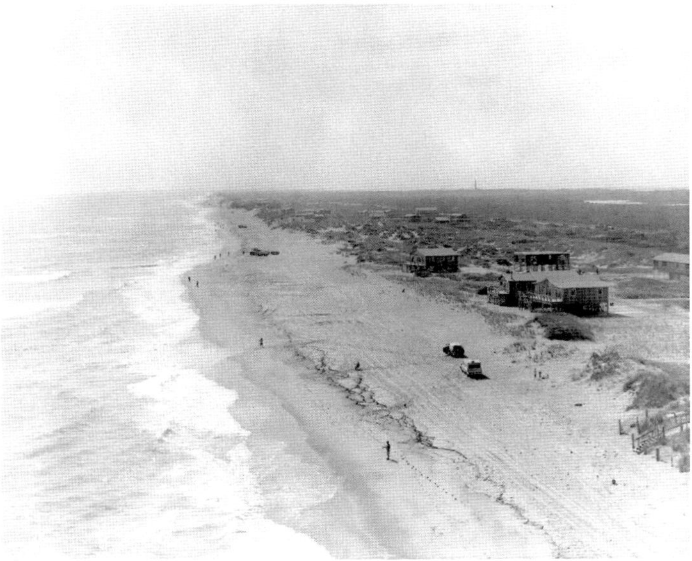

Anglers in South Nags Head. The Oregon Inlet Bridge and Bodie Island Lighthouse are visible in the background. *Photo by Aycock Brown, Outer Banks History Center, circa 1960.*

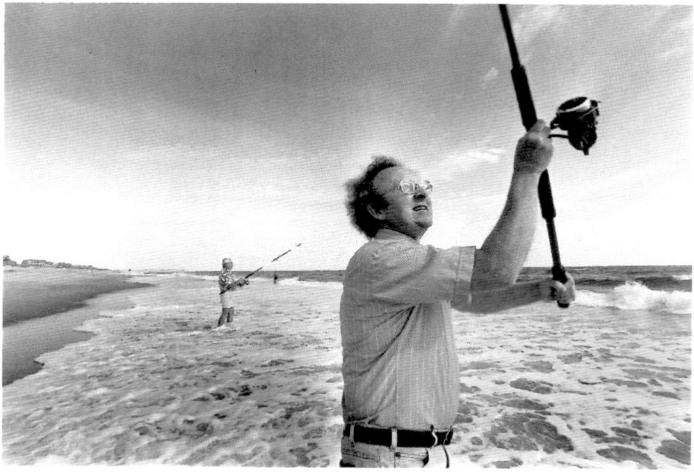

Jack Herrington and Damon Tatem cast south of the Nags Head pier. In 1974, while fishing out of Oregon Inlet, Herrington, of Allison Park, Pennsylvania, was the first man in the world to land a blue marlin weighing over one thousand pounds. Tatem ran Tatem's Tackle Box across from Jockey's Ridge from 1971 to 1998 and is also known for his fishing columns. *Photo by Drew C. Wilson, Outer Banks History Center, 1993.*

Chapter 6

# OUR SURFING CULTURE

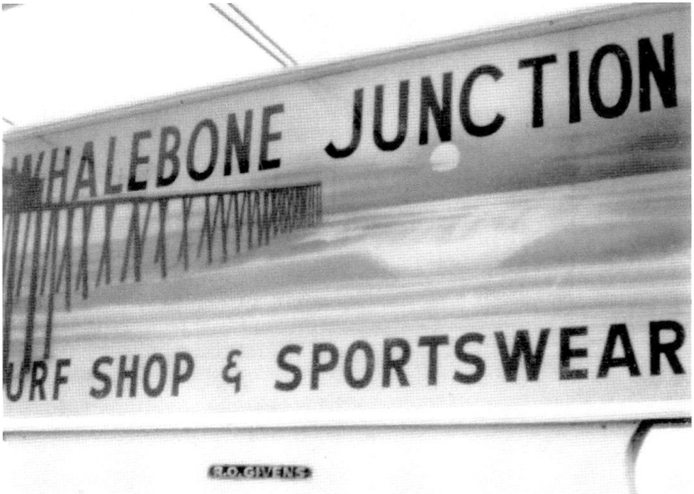


Whalebone Junction Surf Shop opened in 1975 as Resincraft. Jim Vaughn bought out his partner the following year and changed the name to reflect the shop's location. *Courtesy Whalebone Surf Shop, circa 1976.*

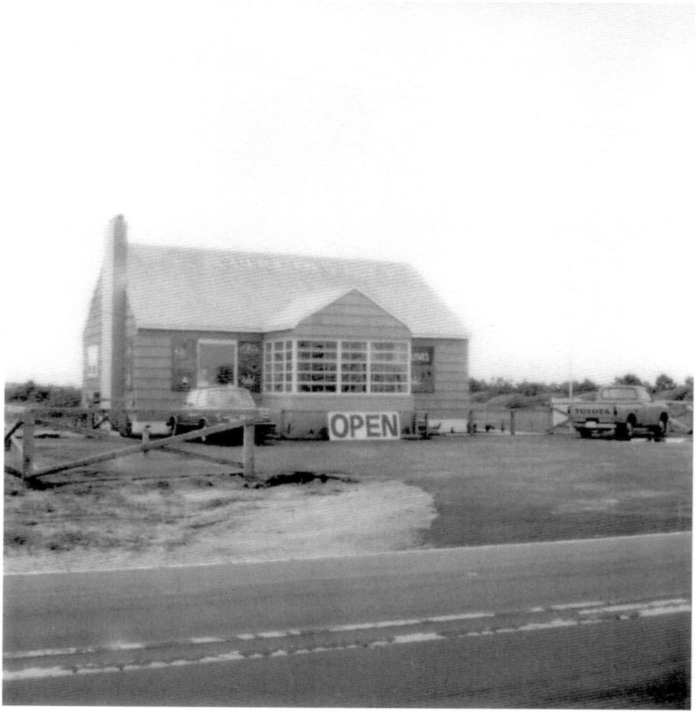


The original Whalebone Junction Surf Shop. *Courtesy Whalebone Surf Shop, circa 1976.*

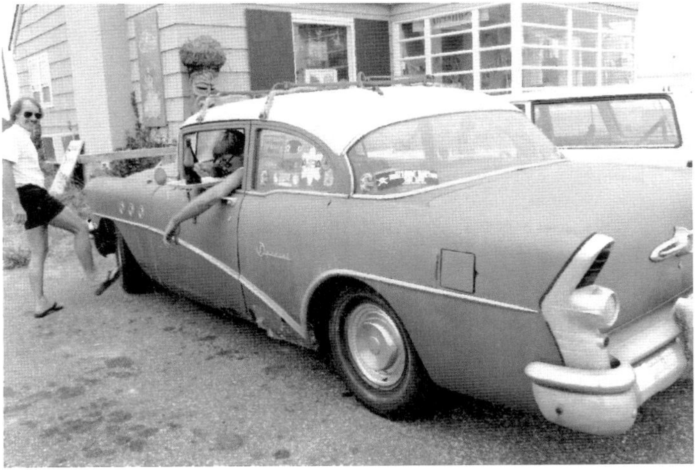

Jim Vaughn and Jim Plimpton in front of Whalebone Junction Surf Shop. Plimpton made surfing movies that were shown at the Catholic church next door to the store. *Courtesy Whalebone Surf Shop, circa 1975.*

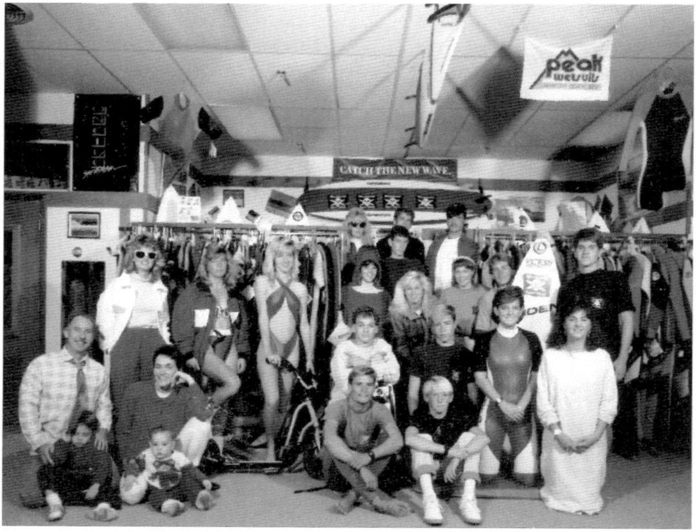


Jim and April Vaughn and family (far left) and the Whalebone Surf Shop staff in their Outer Banks Mall location. *Courtesy Whalebone Surf Shop, 1986.*

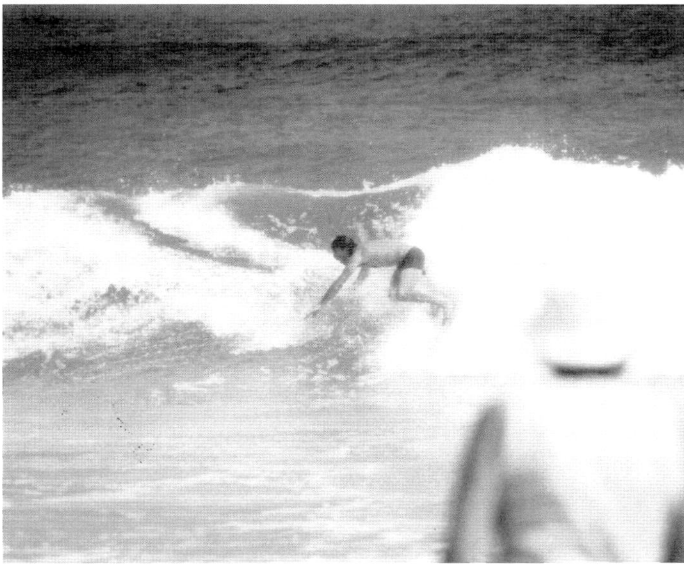

Steve Hess at Nags Head Pier. The Norfolk native began surfing and developed an interest in shaping boards in the late 1960s. *Courtesy Secret Spot Surf Shop, 1980.*

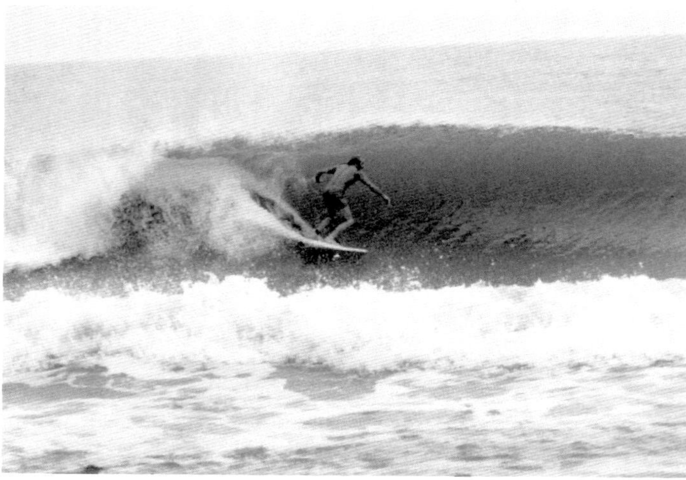

Mike Sieloff charges an overhead wave north of Nags Head Pier. *Photo by Steve Hess, courtesy Secret Spot Surf Shop, 1985.*

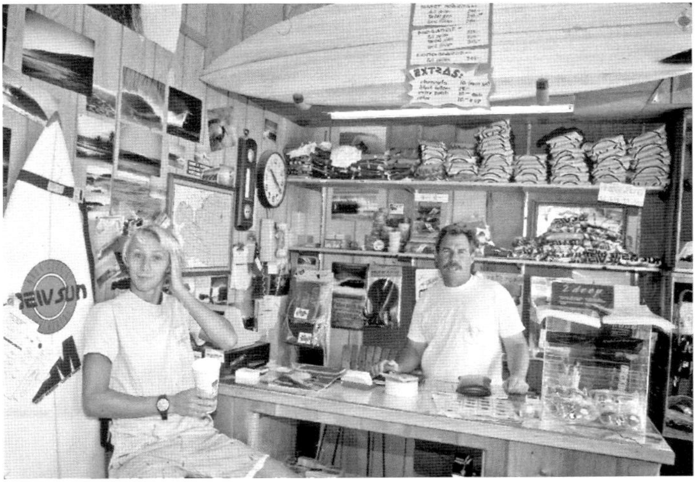


Rascoe Hunt and New Sun founder Mickey McCarthy in front of the New Sun Shop. *Photo by Tom Dugan,* Eastern Surf Magazine, *circa 1984.*

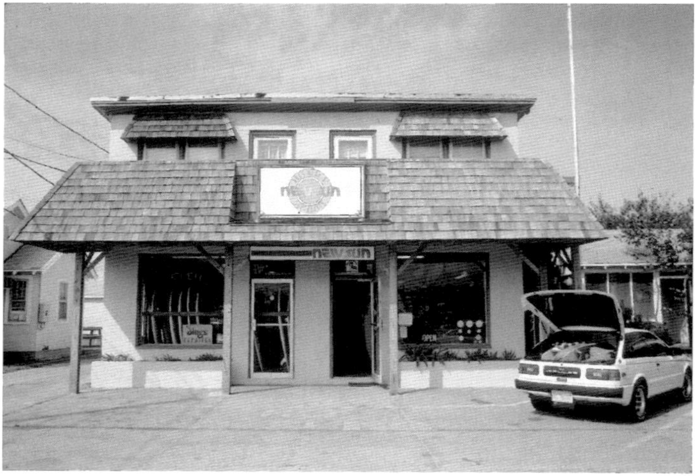

New Sun Surf Shop on the Beach Road across from Nags Head Pier.
*Photo by Tom Dugan,* Eastern Surf Magazine, *circa 1984.*

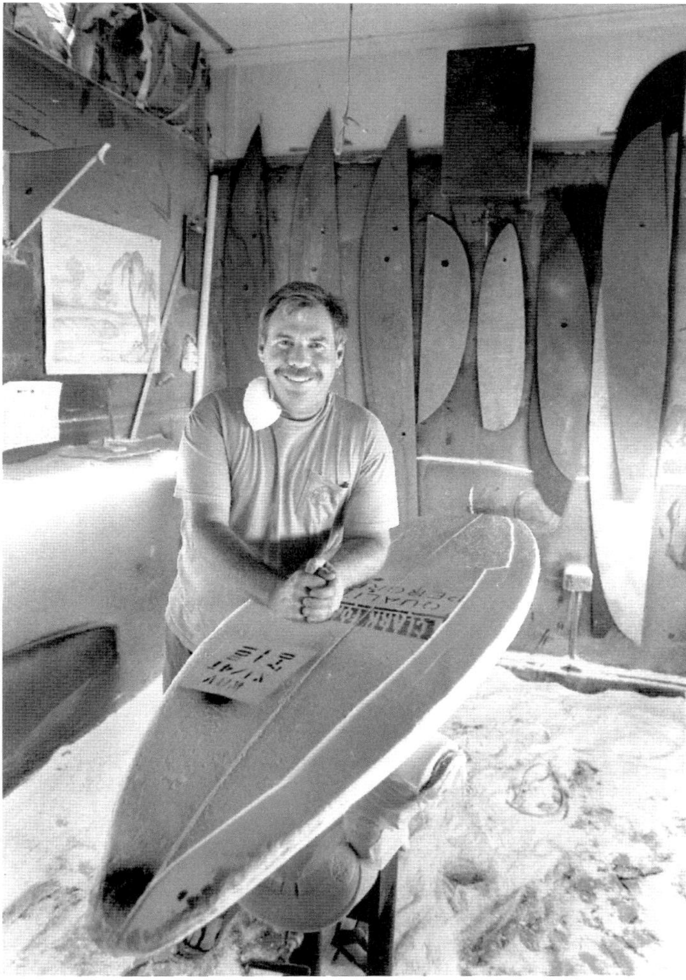

Mickey McCarthy in the New Sun shaping room. *Photo by Drew C. Wilson, Outer Banks History Center, 1989.*

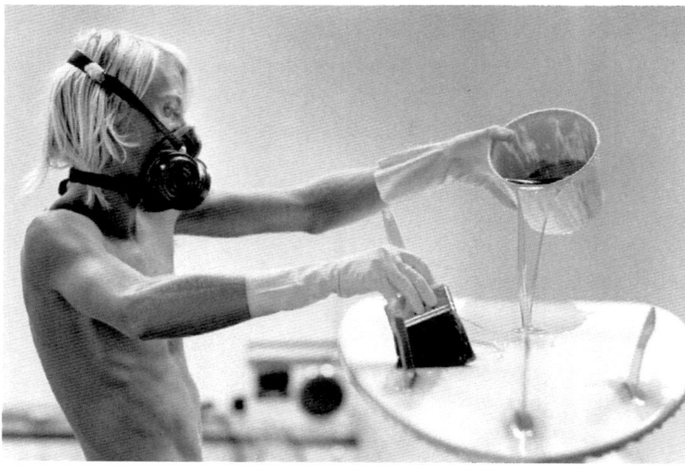

Rascoe Hunt of New Sun Surfboards glasses a triple fin board. *Photo by Drew C. Wilson, Outer Banks History Center, 1990.*

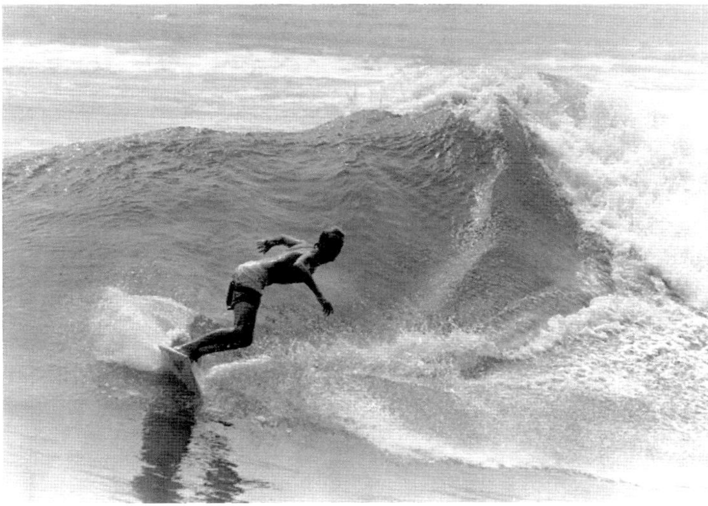

An unknown surfer rides the swell from Hurricane Bertha south of Nags Head Pier. In addition to breaks north and south of Nags Head Pier, early surf spots included south of the old Carolinian Hotel in front of the old Planter's Bank building as well as "the domes" across from the geodesic dome house at the end of South Nags Head. *Photo by Drew C. Wilson, Outer Banks History Center, 1990.*

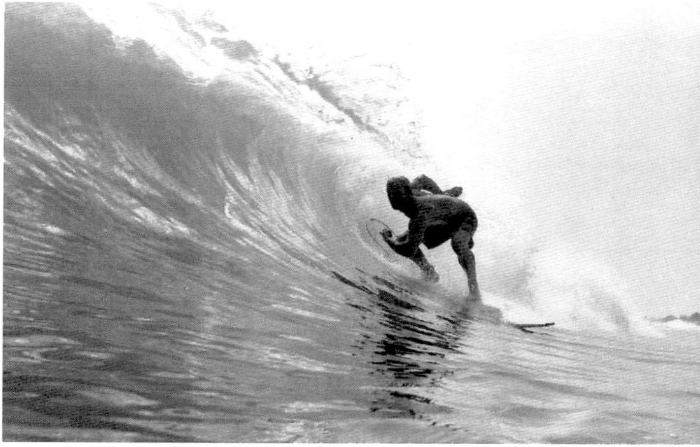

Jodie Millen in the curl of a Nags Head wave. *Photo by Drew C. Wilson, Outer Banks History Center, 1993.*

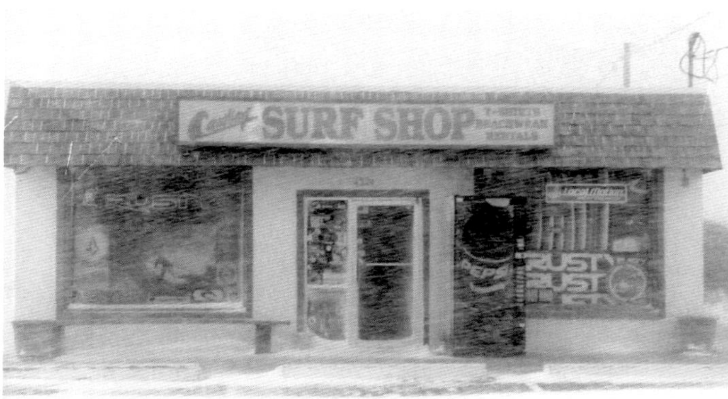


Cavalier Surf Shop captured in a Nags Head snow. *Courtesy Cavalier Surf Shop, circa 2002.*

## Chapter 7

# THE STEADFAST AND STALWART

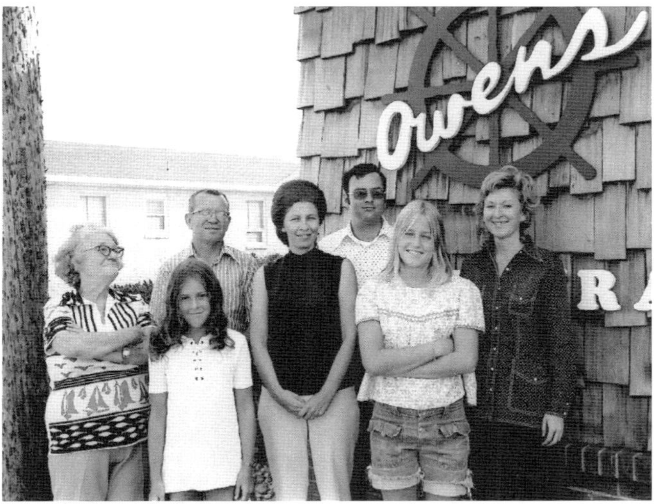


After breaking into the restaurant business in Manteo, Robert and Clara Owens decided to venture over to the beach and opened the twenty-four-seat Owens' Café and a small hostelry, Owens' Motel, in 1947. The restaurant, the oldest on the Outer Banks continuously owned by one family, is considered by many the pièce de résistance. The Owens and Shannon families standing in front of Owens' Restaurant, which has become a Nags Head institution. *Photo by J. Foster Scott, Outer Banks History Center, 1973.*

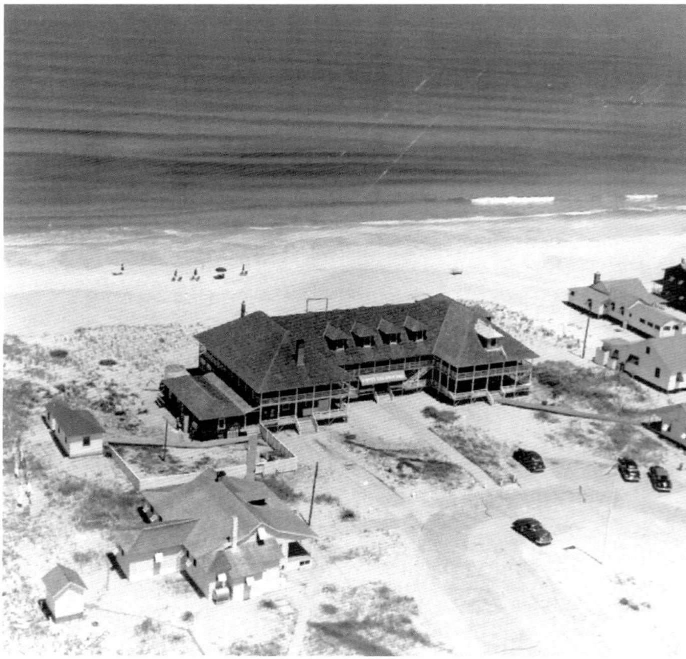

The First Colony Inn opened on the oceanfront across from Jockey's Ridge in 1932, after the completion of the Wright Memorial Bridge and the building of the Virginia Dare Trail opened the beaches to automobile traffic in 1930. Henry and Marie LeRoy from Elizabeth City were the inn's first owners and called the three-story hotel LeRoy's Seaside Inn. In 1937, new owners C.P. Midgett and Ernest Jones capitalized on the area's latest attraction, *The Lost Colony*, and changed the name to First Colony Inn. *Photo by Roger P. Meekins, Outer Banks History Center, 1950.*

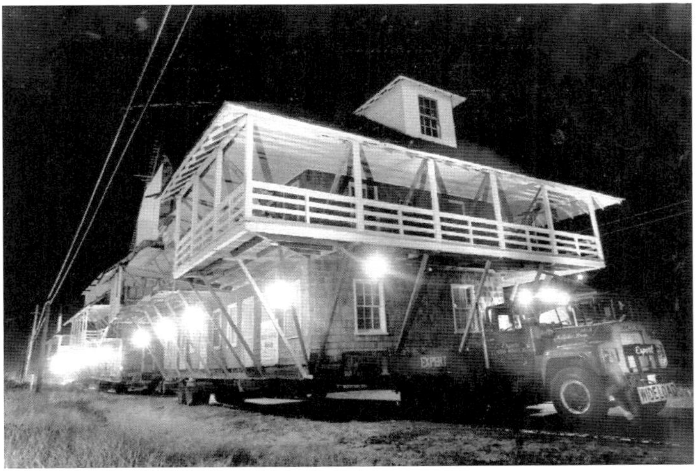

By the late 1980s, the First Colony Inn had been threatened by erosion on several occasions and was in need of a face-lift if it was to remain a viable hostelry. Richard and Camille Lawrence purchased the inn, and in August 1988 the structure was divided into three sections and relocated between the highways three and a half miles south of its original location. It has been lovingly refurbished and continues to welcome visitors who are able to experience the timeless grace in its simple yet elegant design. *Photo by Drew C. Wilson, Outer Banks History Center, 1988.*

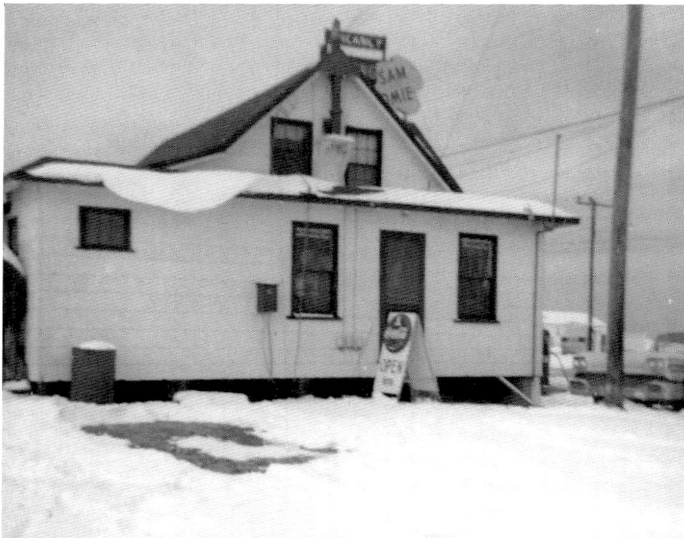


In 1937, Captain Sambo Tillett opened a small restaurant near Whalebone Junction where captains would meet for breakfast before taking out their daily fishing charters and then again to compare notes about the day's catch. *Courtesy Sam and Omie's, circa 1957.*

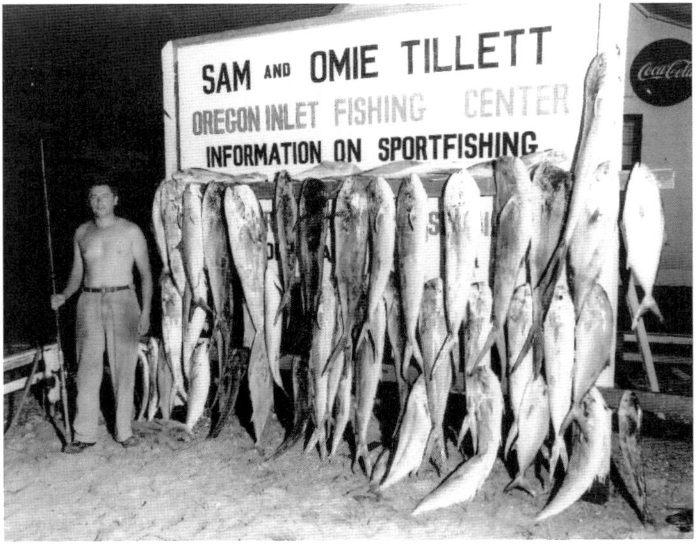


In time, trips were booked directly from the restaurant. Tillett also brought his son into the business, which became known as Sam and Omie's. The restaurant has changed ownership over the years, but the nondescript cedar-shaked building continues as one of Nags Head's most popular watering holes. *Photo by Aycock Brown, Outer Banks History Center, 1954.*

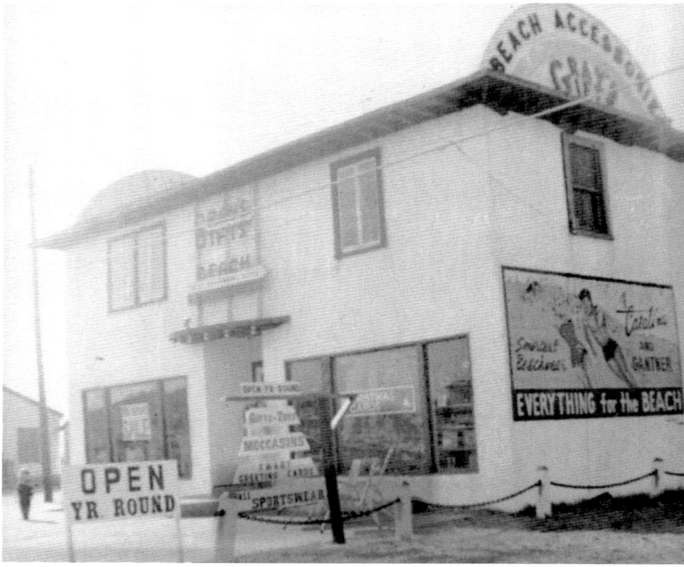


Walter and Estelle Gray opened Gray's Gifts and Beach Accessories in 1948. The two-story concrete building had a shop downstairs that sold beach gear and sundries to vacationers, while the Grays and their five children lived above. Although the Nags Head store closed years ago, the business continues as Gray's Sportswear in six locations from Corolla to Kitty Hawk. Gray's Sportswear and the Gray family are active supporters of many local causes, such as Surfrider Foundation and the Nags Head Woods Run. The old Beach Road store is now housing for Gray's seasonal employees. *Courtesy Gray's Sportswear, 1956.*

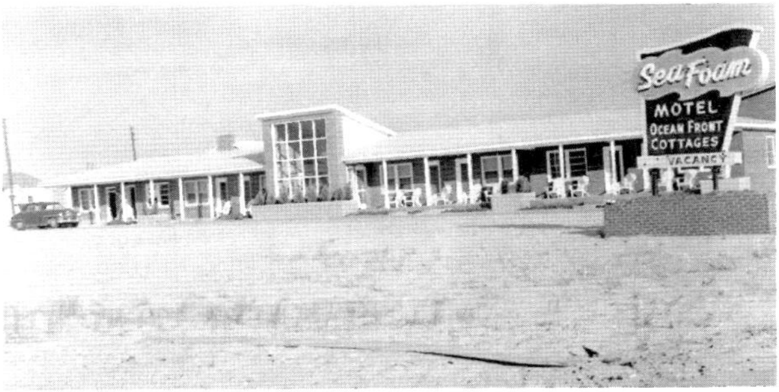


The Sea Foam Motel was built in 1948 and has expanded over the years. It is listed on the National Register of Historic Places. *Photo by Aycock Brown, Outer Banks History Center, 1954.*

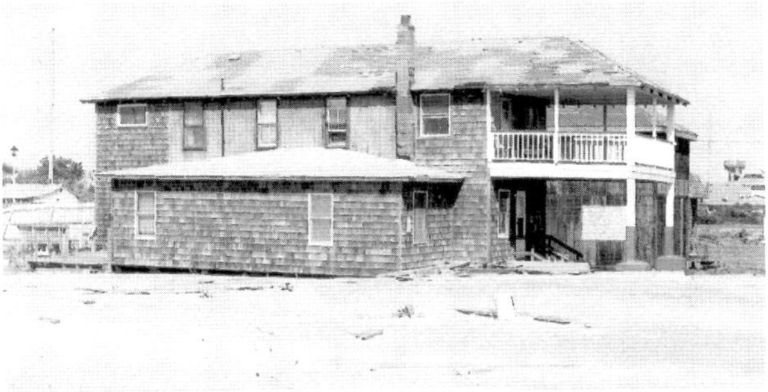

Midgett's Store was built in 1914 on the sound side and moved to its present Beach Road location after the 1933 hurricane. Mattie Midgett ran the store. Her husband, Jethro, was a fisherman. Jethro Jr. delivered ice to summer people and was admired by many a young girl. The Midgetts' daughter, Nellie Myrtle, was the Outer Banks' preeminent beachcomber and walked the beach daily, collecting all that the sea offered. Her collection is housed in the old store as the Beachcomber Museum. This image is of the store after Hurricane Isabel. *Photo by Chaz Winkler, Beachcomber Museum, 2003.*

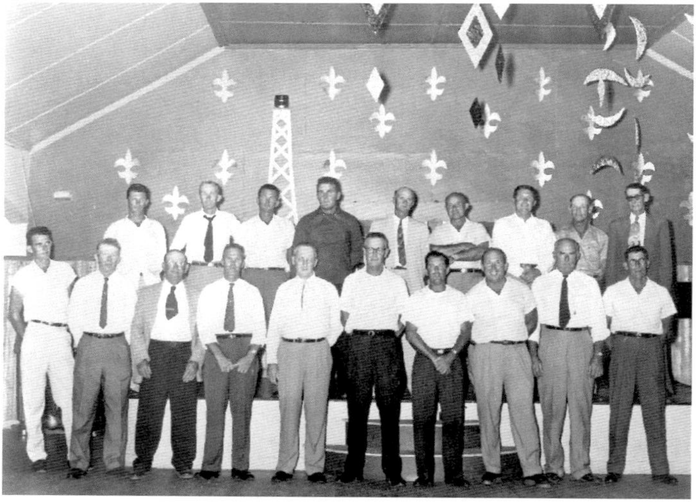

Many local events took place at the Shrine Club at Whalebone Junction. Dinners were held there, and *The Lost Colony* cast would perform after its shows at Waterside Theater. Charter boat captains assembled at the Dare County Shrine Club. *First row, left to right*: Carson Stallings's son-in-law, Will Etheridge Jr., Jesse Etheridge, Moon Tillett, Fred Basnight, Ken Ward, Harry Baum, Matt Spivey, Dan Lewark, Warren O'Neal. *Second row, left to right*: Billy Baum, H.T. Gaskins, Omie Tillett, Charles Scarborough, Warren Gallop, Carson Stallings, Charles Midgett, Wayland Baum, Clarence Holmes. *Photo by Aycock Brown, Outer Banks History Center, circa 1957.*

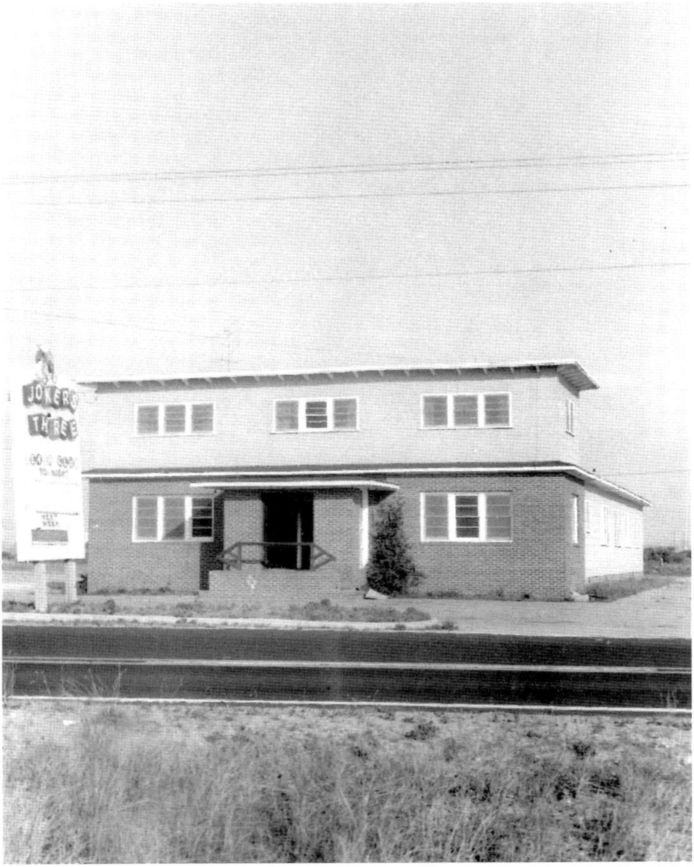


For a few years during the 1960s, the Shrine Club became Joker's Three Beach Club, which featured live music and dancing. Since the 1970s, the building has been Holy Trinity Catholic Church, which now offers bilingual Mass. *Photo by Aycock Brown, Outer Banks History Center, 1967.*

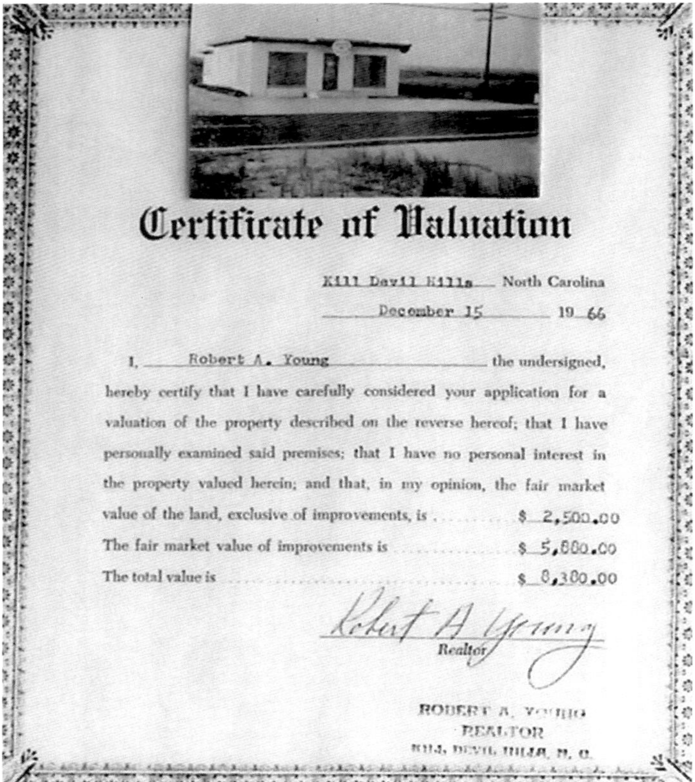

Certificate of Valuation

Kill Devil Hills North Carolina

December 15 19 66

I, Robert A. Young the undersigned, hereby certify that I have carefully considered your application for a valuation of the property described on the reverse hereof; that I have personally examined said premises; that I have no personal interest in the property valued herein; and that, in my opinion, the fair market value of the land, exclusive of improvements, is . . . . . . . . . $ 2,500.00

The fair market value of improvements is . . . . . . . . . $ 5,880.00

The total value is . . . . . . . . . $ 8,380.00

Robert A Young
Realtor

ROBERT A. YOUNG
REALTOR
KILL DEVIL HILLS, N. C.

Chester and Barbara Smith began Seaside Art Gallery in 1961, when they leased a small building on the Beach Road that was once an antiques store. It was one of the first retail shops in Nags Head and was only open three months during the year. Mrs. Smith was an artist, and at that time there were no places to display and sell art. The Smiths purchased the building for around $8,000 and added on over the years. Today the shop is managed by the Smiths' daughter, Melanie. *Courtesy Seaside Art Gallery, circa 1966.*

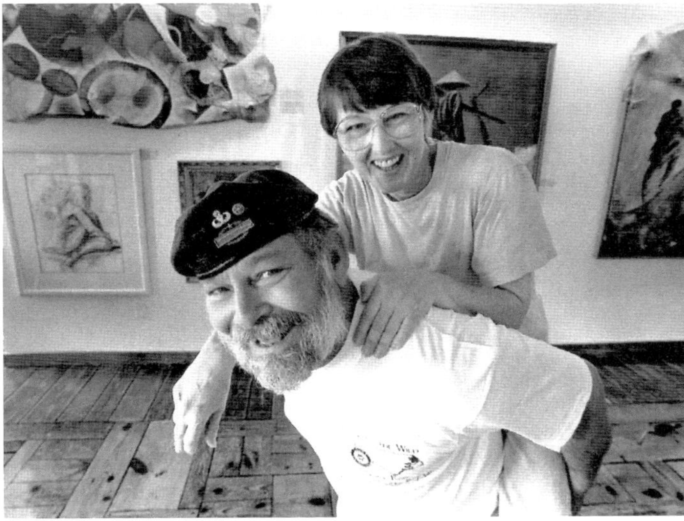

Glenn and Pat Eure have been active in the local arts community for thirty years. In 1977, Glenn, a printmaker, opened a small shop in the Beach Mart Shopping Center in Kill Devil Hills and later opened the Ghost Fleet Gallery on Gallery Row in Nags Head in 1982. Since that time, the Eures have hosted scores of exhibits, the annual Frank Stick Memorial Art Show and the annual Dare County Schools Art Exhibit. The gallery has been used for social gatherings, church services, weddings and even a funeral. *Photo by Drew C. Wilson, Outer Banks History Center, 1992.*

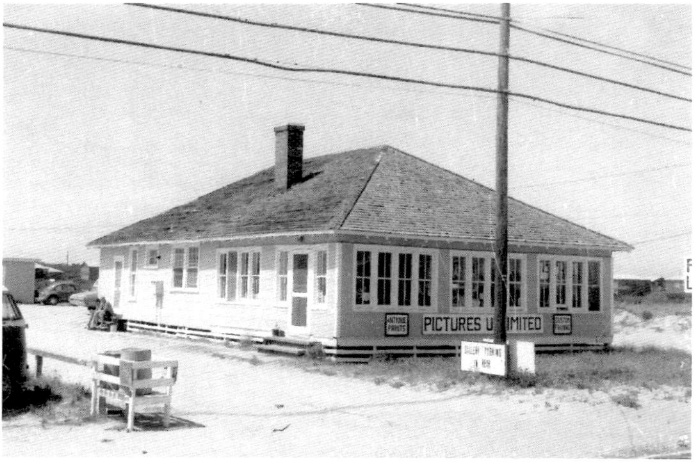

Jack Sandberg, aka "Uncle Jack," moved to the Outer Banks from Pittsburgh after a rewarding teaching career. In 1969, he and his wife ran a small gallery at the First Colony Inn. After seven years, the gallery moved to a 1935 cottage near the intersection of Barnes Street and the Beach Road. In 1977, it opened as Pictures Unlimited and became the Yellowhouse Gallery the following year. *Courtesy Jack Sandberg, 1977.*

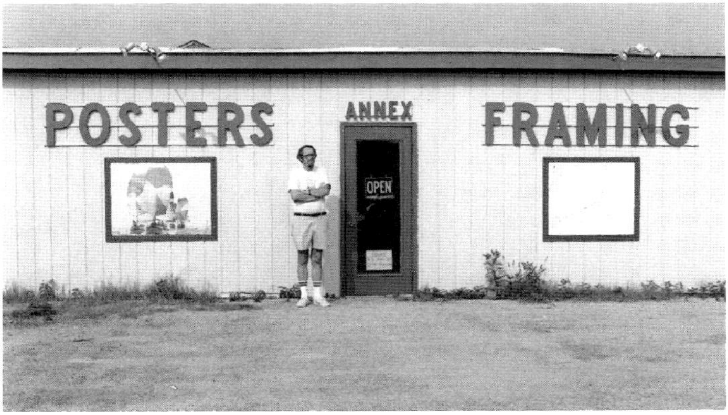


While Yellowhouse Gallery offered antique prints, maps and the like, behind the building was the Yellowhouse Annex, which featured posters and prints. Jack also did framing in the Annex and would gladly offer a free cat with any purchase. In addition to running the Yellowhouse, Uncle Jack also wrote a popular and pithy column for the *Outer Banks Current* and later the *Outer Banks Sentinel*. In 2006, Eve and Pete Turek purchased the Yellowhouse, and they still continue the legacy. *Courtesy Jack Sandberg, circa 1984.*

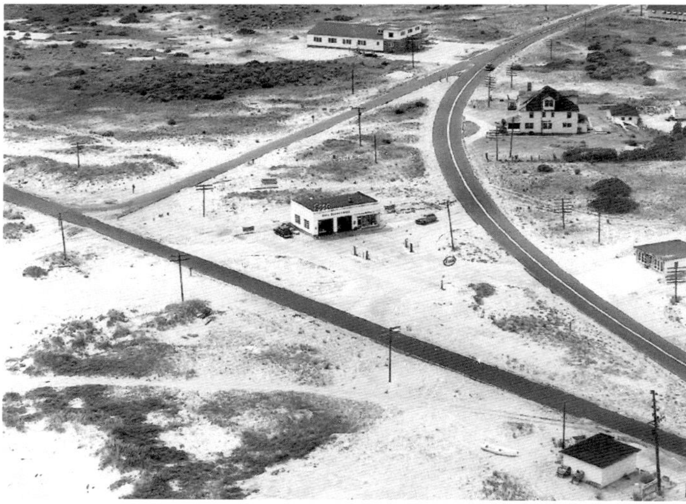

Manteo's Moncie Daniels built three Esso service stations along the Beach Road in the 1950s: one across from Jockey's Ridge (now Sooey's BBQ), one in Kitty Hawk and one at Whalebone Junction to replace the earlier Whalebone station, which is said to have burned down. Walter B. Gray Jr. (no relation to Walter Gray of Gray's Department Store) ran the Jockey's Ridge Station for a number of years. This image is of the Whalebone Esso Station at Whalebone Junction, with the Sea Rest Tourist Home and the Shrine Club in the background. *Photo by Roger P. Meekins, Outer Banks History Center, circa 1954.*

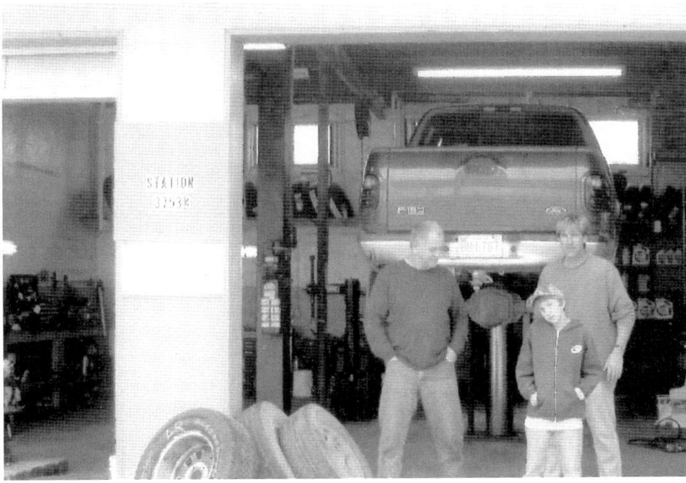

Walter B. "Wally" Gray III, whose father ran Jockey's Ridge Esso, has operated the Whalebone gas station since 1976. This image depicts three generations of Grays—Wally, his son Jeff and grandson Jeffrey. *Photo by author, 2008.*

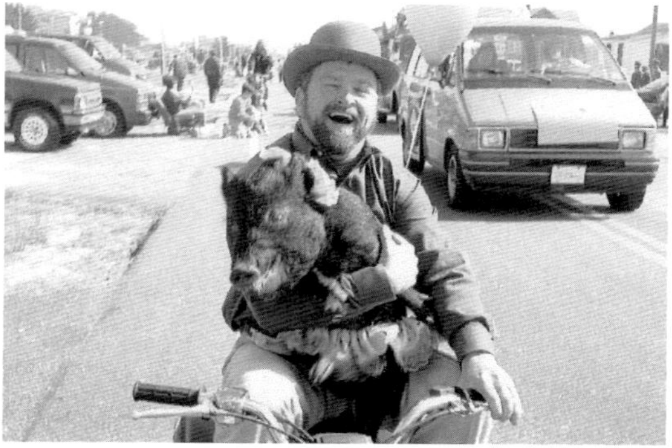

Nags Head restaurateur Mike Kelly came up through the culinary and hospitality ranks working for Mike Hayman at the Sea Fare Restaurant. He opened Kelly's Restaurant and Tavern in 1985, which had run a short stint as J. Fleming Munde's. In 1990, Kelly started the Kelly's St. Patrick's Day Parade as a fun way to help establish a community identity. *Photo by Bob Furr, courtesy Kelly's Outer Banks Restaurant and Tavern, circa 1996.*

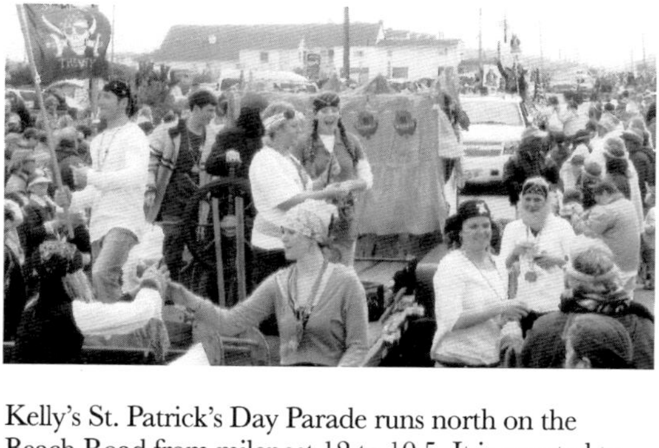

Kelly's St. Patrick's Day Parade runs north on the Beach Road from milepost 12 to 10.5. It is reputed to be the largest parade in North Carolina. *Photo by Bob Furr, courtesy Kelly's Outer Banks Restaurant and Tavern, 2008.*

# FOR FURTHER READING


Bishir, Catherine W. *The "Unpainted Aristocracy": The Beach Cottages of Old Nags Head.* Raleigh: Division of Archives and History, North Carolina Department of Cultural Resources, 1978.

Jones, Lu Anne, and Amy Glass. *"Everyone Helped His Neighbor": Memories of Nags Head Woods.* Kill Devil Hills, NC: Nature Conservancy, Nags Head Woods Preserve, 1987.

Outlaw, Edward Ralph. *Old Nag's Head: Personal Recollections and Some History of the Region in North Carolina at the Edge of the Sea Where Our First Colonists Landed.* Norfolk, VA: Liskey Lithograph Corp., 1956.

Rountree, Susan Byrum. *Nags Headers.* Winston-Salem, NC: John F. Blair, 2001.

Seaworthy, Gregory. *Nag's Head, or, Two Months among "The Bankers" a Story of Sea-shore Life and Manners.* Philadelphia: A. Hart, 1850.

Stick, David. *The Outer Banks of North Carolina, 1584–1958.* Chapel Hill: University of North Carolina Press, 1958.

———. *People to Preserve Jockey's Ridge, 1973–1980.* Unpublished manuscript held at the Outer Banks History Center, Manteo, North Carolina.